A Beginning Singer's Guide

Richard Davis

The Scarecrow Press, Inc.
Lanham, Maryland, and Oxford
1998

SCARECROW PRESS, INC.

Published in the United States of America
by Scarecrow Press, Inc.
4720 Boston Way
Lanham, Maryland 20706

4 Pleydell Gardens, Folkestone
Kent CT20 2DN, England

British Library Cataloguing in Publication Information Available

Library of Congress Cataloging-in-Publication Data

Davis, Richard, 1951–
    A beginning singer's guide / Richard Davis.
       p.   cm.
    Includes bibiliographical references (p. 193) and index.
    ISBN 0-8108-3555-X (alk. paper). — ISBN 0-8108-3556-8 (pbk.:
alk. paper)
      1. Singing—Instruction and study. I. Title.
MT820.D27   1998
783'.014—dc21   98-8656
                                            CIP
                                            MN

TO BETSY AND CAROLINE

Contents

Figures

Tables

Preface

Twenty years ago, when I first started teaching singers for pay, I began the first lesson with a new student in this way. I handed the student a sheet of lined paper and asked him or her to write answers to the following questions:

Why does humankind sing?
Why do you want to sing?
How do you think you learn how to sing?

In order to let the student think without distraction, I left the room for ten minutes, saying we would consider the answers upon my return. When I got back I discovered that my new student had either written a long series of answers to my questions or returned to me a blank sheet of paper accompanied by an even blanker stare. In either case I went over what I considered to be the best answers to the questions with my student.

Humankind has always sung. Primitives used phonation to communicate emotional states before they began to develop speech, just as babies do now. Primitive mothers most probably intoned some kind of tune to get their babies to sleep, and primitive man had his hunting cries and groans of grief when a friend was lost in the hunt. Singing has a long historical precedent. It is, if we consider its primitive intonations, the root of our communication with one another. Whether it be Bantu war chants or German Lieder, singing is communicating.

The best reasons for wanting to sing are those that express a humanistic altruism. We should sing because it is a gift God gave to us and expects us to use. We should sing because we feel we have a special way of communicating or a special message to communicate to others. We should sing because it makes us and our hearers happy. We should sing because communicating the thoughts and feelings of other sensitive souls helps us all to better understand the human condition.

I have been told unabashedly by some of my students that fame and fortune was the well-spring of their desire to sing. I believe that this motivation, although typical of our selfish and materialistic age, will not lead to the development of character or empathy in a singer.

Singers learn to sing—or develop a technique, as we call it in the discipline—by methods that in large measure are unique to that individual student. No one method of learning to sing serves all students equally well because every voice is a law unto itself. While we are all anatomically related to one another, our physical sensations in response to the singing act and our intellectual responses to empirical and psychological directives differ widely among individuals. It is for this reason that most teachers of singing present themselves as guides and facilitators rather than omniscient gurus. A teacher can help you learn to sing, but much of what the student learns is specific to himself or herself. It is for this reason, I believe, that some famous and egocentric singers routinely tell the press that they are "self-taught."

After administering this little pop quiz on the first day of class, I was always surprised to note that despite their unprepossessing beginning in my studio, those students who handed in the blank sheets of paper usually turned out to be as proficient in singing as their more articulate peers. My unscientific explanation for why this was so is based on the idea that motivation, spoken or unspoken, analyzed or unanalyzed, is the key factor to success in any endeavor. We are all a collection of motivating preferences which shape a worldview. In due course, that worldview shapes the conduct of our lives. As a student of singing, your worldview must encompass the motivations implied in those three questions. Without them, you will not have the will to practice, the desire to comprehend, or the ability to communicate through song.

How to Use This Book

This book is designed for four practical uses. First, it can be used as a collateral text for studio voice lessons. Rather than spend precious lesson time explaining the mechanism and culture of singing, your teacher will assign reading in this book. He or she may elect to hand you a worksheet to review your reading (see sample in chapter 7), or answer your questions in the next lesson. Your teacher may ask you to complete a song/aria study guide to enrich your understanding of song assignments (see form in chapter 7). Vocal progress will be faster because the lesson time is spent singing instead of talking. The process of singing will be easier to understand because it has been presented in a sequential narrative. Second, many students take a one-term course in vocal pedagogy as undergraduates. The population of this course is likely to be voice students and future choral conductors. A special chapter for the future choral conductor containing methods and other helps should meet the need for an all-in-one text for this class. Third, it can be used as a practical guide for new voice teachers. A special chapter containing methods and studio administration helps will be very useful to the new teacher of voice. Fourth, the text can serve as a reference for those interested in areas of vocal pedagogy not covered in other books. Working with a pianist, improving memory, acting, interpretation, and alleviating performance anxiety all are discussed. These important, often disregarded skills, can make the difference in a singer's success or failure.

Acknowledgments

The author thanks Edgar Smith for the anatomical illustrations; Art Reidel for the musical illustrations; and my colleagues Wanda Brister, Richard Kennedy, and Lynne Garrett for making helpful comments about the contents of this book. Many thanks to the editors of the *Journal of Singing,* the *Choral Journal,* and the *American Music Teacher* for allowing the substance of my articles to be used here.

Chapter 1

Musical Styles of Singing

After deciding to invest both time and resources toward the study of singing, a student must choose what musical style most interests him or her and find a teacher who is willing to teach it. Right? Wrong. This very logical, consumer-oriented approach is practiced by many students to their detriment, for the following reasons:

1. Studying only the music you like to sing fails to broaden both your technical facility and your artistic horizons. Musicians should not be like the man in the art museum who blithely says he knows nothing about art, but knows what he likes. How can an intelligent person possibly know his or her artistic preferences without knowing about the technique used to create a work, without knowing about the life and times of the artist who created it, or without knowing about how this work differs from other works in the genre. One can be attracted to something for reasons beyond articulation, but one can never love something without understanding it.

2. Studying only the music you prefer to sing leaves you one-dimensional as a performer. The reason crossover stars are so admired is that they have mastered effective communication in more than one style,

thus becoming more universal in their appeal to the
public. While it is true that most people are given to
chuckle when they hear Pavarotti attempt a pop tune
in English, fewer people are laughing when they hear
Amy Grant on the Top 40 or listen to Barbra Streisand when she goes classical.
3. Singing in only one style can actually damage the
voice. Witness the fact that rock musicians very often
end their careers with literally a whisper of the voice
they once had.

To be truly effective, vocal study must cover a broad range of musical styles and performing parameters. It is the only way a student's
true talents can be identified and cultivated. The basic vocal styles and
some of the components, musical and amusical, that form them will
follow.

Classical singing includes recital, oratorio, opera, operetta, and traditional church music. Its usual musical attributes are common-practice
harmony with long, wide-ranging, often tessitura-sensitive musical
phrases. Melodies may be stepwise or contain wide leaps. The vocal
lines often come from a rather complex harmonic web that requires har-
monically independent singing. The musical aesthetic in this genre demands that the interpreter realize the intentions of the composer before
acknowledging his or her own. Music is performed, at least when compared to rock, with very little physical movement, but much inner intensity. Music is often performed in the original language to preserve
the integrity of poetry of high literary profile. This music is most always performed in a formal setting of some kind. The history of this
genre of vocal performance goes all the way back to ancient Greece and
continues to enjoy robust performance in Europe and America.

Popular style includes a wide variety of musical styles whose vocal
stylings differ most in the way words are articulated. It includes folk,
country and western, blues, standards, Christian rock, rock, hard rock
(heavy metal), and eclectic popular stylings too numerous to mention.
Harmony and melody are both subjugated to rhythm in the rock section
of this genre, with standards and folk sounding more like what we
would expect in classical singing. Melodic types in popular style are
usually very simple. Songs are composed with a "hook," a melodic or
harmonic fragment that makes the piece easily identifiable and distinct
upon second hearing. Commercialism demands that a tune be

memorable—you don't buy what you don't remember. Phrase lengths most often are short, sometimes composed of just a single word. Ranges may be very wide (Mariah Carey), or more usually very narrow. Wide-ranging tunes generally rely on a vocal gimmick like falsetto or whistle register. Songs are not tessitura-sensitive since they are often molded more to the particular technique of the performer/songwriter than to a specific voice type. This style allows any and all types of language usage, from poetry to blank verse to nonsense. The aesthetic of this genre is founded upon the idea of emotional, high-profile communication by whatever means seem appropriate to that communication. A head banger may destroy his guitar or eat a rat if he feels it is necessary to his or her expression. The communicative freedom expressed by this genre can result in the poorest of vocal hygiene. "Packaging" of the performer is very important to being able to "sell" his product to the public. Madonna changes her image on a regular basis to keep the public interested in her. Performance venues are most often supplied through mechanical venues—tapes, CDs, and television (MTV, etc.). Because the venue is mechanical, it is not unusual to witness lip-synching, incredible histrionics while singing, and lots of mechanical doctoring of the singing itself. The history of this kind of music is relatively short when compared to classical music, and in its current incarnation in America, of fleeting interest to the public. The average chart tune becomes a golden oldie in less than a year. Financial reward in this area of singing can be phenomenal.

Music for the theatre includes music for the Broadway stage, movie adaptations of stage shows, and original movie musicals. Harmony is always from the common practice period. Melodies may be dominated by word rhythms and narrow ranged (Sondheim), or memorable diatonic tunes with fairly wide range (Gershwin). Most of the music, like the stage roles themselves, is for a particular type of personality and voice. The musical aesthetic is dependent upon the tune's context in the show. A particular type of vocalism called belt is often employed. Belt was particularly important when most theatres' performances were not amplified. Ethel Merman is the usual example cited for this type of vocalism. Theatre music has accommodated a wide range of vocal stylings from belt (*Annie*), legitimate (*Sound of Music*), and eclectic styles blending opera, pop, and theatre styles (*Hair, Phantom of the Opera*). This style is most always associated with live performance. The history of this style begins with *The Black Crook* in 1866.

Of the three styles noted, the classical style is the one most widely taught in this country. The reasons for that are fairly obvious. Both pop and theatre styles require less vocal tutoring to achieve professional status. In fact, often no tutoring is required. Artists in these genres strive for naturalness, although the means to achieve that goal may often be quite unnatural. Singing teachers, regardless of their advertised affinity, are likely to be classically trained, and strictly as a matter of preserving the voice over time, may teach a classical technique to their students regardless of which musical style the student is interested in. The majority of voice teachers in this country are employed by educational institutions that stress a broad, historically based, classical training.

Chapter 2

Mechanism and Technique

Vocal Mechanism

The vocal mechanism is an air-column instrument related in theory, and sometimes in morphology, to the brass and woodwind families. Many analogies have been drawn relating the singing mechanism to these instruments, and more colorfully to the workings of cars and other mechanical contrivances. Related in simplified gestalt, here are the steps to singing. Paragraph numbers refer to Figure 2.2.

1. *Impulse.* The brain perceives the sound it wants to make and sends neural impulses through the central nervous system
2. *Respiration.* The eight muscles of inspiration actuate, expanding the thorax and creating low pressure in the lungs to which higher-pressure outside air flows through the mouth, nose, and trachea. The six muscles of expiration begin contracting, and along with the natural elasticity of the lungs, propel air under pressure through the trachea to the vocal folds.
3. *Phonation.* The vocal folds, by a complex muscular activity, approximate (come together) and begin to open and close (cycle or phase) in the passing air column. Pressure from below forces the fold to open, and the Bernoulli effect combined with the tension of the folds pulls them closed again. Puffs of air are pro-

duced by each opening and closing—the number of puffs corresponding to the pitch to be sung. The resulting sound produced by the voice source is much like the sound brass players make when they buzz their lips.

4. & 5. *Resonation/Articulation*. The puffs of air travel through the pharynx, mouth, and in some situations the nose, where a marked change occurs to the sound of the voice source. Because the spectrum of the glottal source is very wide, some partials (vowel formants) are enhanced in strength (resonated) and some are attenuated (filtered out) as they pass through the cavities of the vocal tract. (See Figure 2.1.) The movement of the articulators (jaw, tongue, lips, and soft palate) when combined with the changing shapes of the resonant cavities transforms the voice source, which originally sounded like a buzz, into intelligible speech and song.

By examining each of the five processes we can better understand how the singing mechanism works and how it can be manipulated for artistic expression. Your vocal study, which will require more than knowing how the mechanism works, is put forth as the technique of singing. Acquiring the technique of singing is aimed at:

- Refining breathing strategies
- Discovering the most resonant positions for all the vowels in the vocal tract
- Improving text articulation
- Perfecting your performing and communication skills
- Learning about the broad history and practice of music

Impulse

The will to sing is transferred to the larynx by two branches of the vagus nerve. Their functions are differentiated, and much about them remains unknown. The superior laryngeal branch innervates the muscle responsible for lengthening the folds—the cricothyroid. No other muscle is innervated by this branch, and it is very important for controlling pitch. The recurrent laryngeal nerve is called recurrent because after it splits off the vagus nerve it goes down to into the thorax and returns behind the cricoid cartilage. It is this branch that is responsible for innervating all the other intrinsic larygeal muscles, including agonist antagonist pairs like the posterior cricoarytenoid and lateral cricoarytenoid.

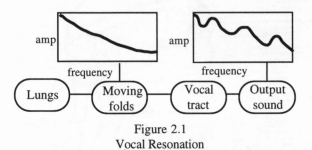

Figure 2.1
Vocal Resonation

Respiration

Posture

The correct posture for singing is necessary so that the vocal organs can be aligned for utmost efficiency. There are as many methods for arriving at this posture as there are singers, but the mental image that most easily aligns the body with the least explanation is to think of a marionette. A string is connected to top of the head, pulling the spine straight up and concomitantly tucking the pelvis directly under the spine. Imagine another string connected to the middle of the chest pulling it slightly up and forward. The basis for this whole posture is provided by a stance with the feet apart the width of the shoulders and one foot slightly ahead of the other. This position keeps the knees from locking, thus preventing a faint, and allowing freedom of movement in all directions.

A second way to feel the noble posture is to stand against a wall with the heels about two to three inches from it. Place the head, shoulders, and buttocks against the wall and try to press the small of the back into the wall, thus tucking the pelvis. Have a friend then gently pull you away from the wall, without moving your feet, so that the weight of the body is directly over the balls of the feet. This feeling of erect posture is what ballet dancers call being centered.

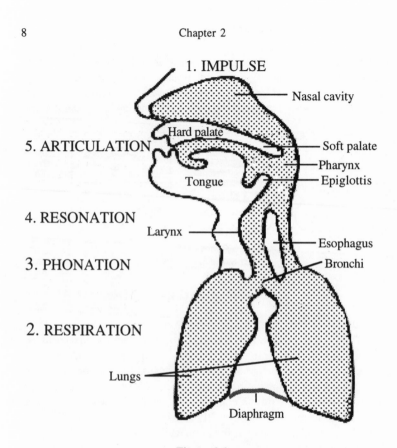

Figure 2.2
Five Processes of Vocal Mechanism

Many generations of singers have subscribed to this old Italian teaching: "The singer should feel small-waisted, barrel-chested, open-throated, and empty headed." I'm sure this old motto is not intended to slur the intelligence of the singer.

Breathing

Breathing for singing is breathing for living. The same mechanism is used, but with slightly modified function. In quiet respiration about 500 milliliters of air are exchanged seventeen times a minute. *Vital capacity* (total lung volume less residual air volume) is about 5 liters in the adult male. Normal respiration is reflexive and involves the following steps:

1. A message from the brain causes the diaphragm to contract pushing the viscera below it out and enlarging the thorax (see Figure 2.3—A expands to B).

2. At the same time the costal muscles (muscles between the ribs) expand the chest in all four directions, concomitantly expanding the lung and dropping the interior air pressure. Higher-pressure exterior air enters to equalize the air pressure.

3. At exhalation, the diaphragm relaxes and the lungs and chest wall recoil, pushing the air out.

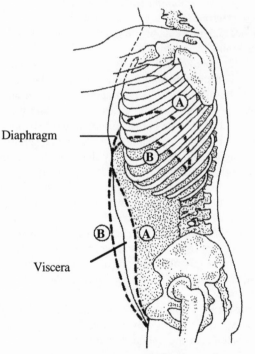

Figure 2.3
Diaphragmatic-Intercostal Breathing
During inhalation the A dotted lines move to B.
During exhalation B moves to A.

Quiet respiration differs from breathing for singing. Breathing for singing requires higher exhalation pressures, larger volumes of air, shorter periods of inhalation, and longer periods of exhalation. These heightened functions are made possible by increasing the size of respiratory movements, increasing or decreasing their speed, and employing agonist/antagonist muscle function to hold the breath and stabilize its pressure. For this reason breathing for singing begins as a learned behavior that will eventually become automatic.

An eminent pedagogue has noted that the systems of breathing for singing—and in fact the aesthetic ideals of singing—vary by country. German singers use predominantly belly breathing, French singers use high chest breathing, and the Italian school (which lately includes most Americans) uses a system combining the positive facets of the other two. This system is referred to as *appoggio* by Italians, even though that word has a broader context than breath management, and diaphragmatic-intercostal breathing by Americans.

Many types of breathing are legitimately taught by voice teachers, and it may be that certain students will find one method of breath management (support) to be more effective than another. It is not uncommon to hear from voice teachers that the efficiency of breath management systems varies with body type or that certain systems work better with certain kinds of singing. It is common for voice teachers to describe fioratura singing as being dominated by diaphragmatic support and soft, sostenuto singing by a sensation of high chest control.

Although many systems of breath management are taught, we will limit our description to the diaphragmatic-intercostal system. It is currently the most mainstream, and most like the one ascribed to by the Italian masters of bel canto. We will describe the structure and function of the breathing mechanism from the bottom up, present a table of the muscles of inspiration and expiration, describe diaphragmatic-intercostal breath management, and include some tips about breathing.

Pelvic Girdle

The pelvic girdle forms a sling that supports the viscera during inhalation and is more energized during exhalation. It is formed by the shape of the pelvis itself and the pelvic diaphragm. The pelvic diaphragm is composed of a pair of muscles, the levator ani, which arise along a line beginning in front of the inner side of the pubic arch and extending along the side wall as far back as the ischial spine. They form the funnel shape at the bottom of the torso where the gut rests. In several methods of breath management the pelvic girdle is forcefully engaged at expiration. The so-called tuck method may use abdominal tuck (engaging the abdominal muscles in a sphincter like maneuver) and pelvic tuck together to push the abdominal diaphragm up. The tuck method may call for the muscles of the buttocks to be tightened during exhalation.

Abdominal Diaphragm

The thoracic diaphragm is probably one of the least understood of all the members of the breathing mechanism. Often one hears "sing from the diaphragm," as though it were a place where tone could be made. One also hears "push the air out with the diaphragm," as if the diaphragm were capable of pushing air anywhere by itself. The diaphragm is a double-domed sheet of muscle with a tendon in the center of it. The right dome is higher than the left on account of the position of the heart above it, and all the muscle fibers attach to the central tendon. The aorta, vena cava, and esophagus pass through the central tendon.

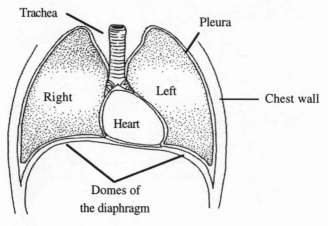

Figure 2.4
Breathing Mechanism

The diaphragm arises from crura (legs) from the first, second and third lumbar vertebrae on the right, and the first and second vertebrae on the left. Additional attachment is made to the costal margin of the lower six ribs and the xiphoid process (tip of the sternum). The excursion of the diaphragm is large. The dome may travel as high as the fifth inter-

costal space when relaxed and as low as the bottom of the ribs when
tensed (6 to 7 centimeters). When the diaphragm contracts it draws the
posterior part of the central tendon down and forward. This flattening of
the domes pushes the viscera below the diaphragm out to form a bulge
called the epigastrium. The flattening also increases the vertical space of
the pleural cavity and moves the costal margins (the inner sides of the
lower ribs) out so that the diameter of the chest is increased. The contraction of the diaphragm brings air in. To exhale, the diaphragm is relaxed and the abdominal muscles below it contract pushing the viscera
in and up against the diaphragm. In a balanced exhalation, the one used
by singers, the strong in and up movement created by the abdominal
muscles is balanced against the down and out movement of the contracting diaphragm for smooth breath flow. The action of the diaphragm
is responsible for most of the increased volume of a deep inspiration.

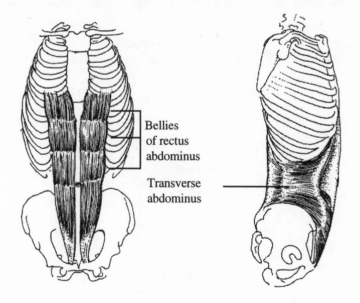

Bellies
of rectus
abdominus

Transverse
abdominus

Figure 2.5
Rectus Abdominus and Transverse Abdominus
The rectus abdominus is one of the strongest muscles in the body.
Its division into bellies or sections allows the muscle to work as a
whole or in sections. This is the muscle you see at work in belly

dancers and muscle builders' "six-pack bellies." The transverse abdominus interdigitates with the rectus abdominus and goes around the abdomen like a barrel. Both work to compress the thorax and viscera.

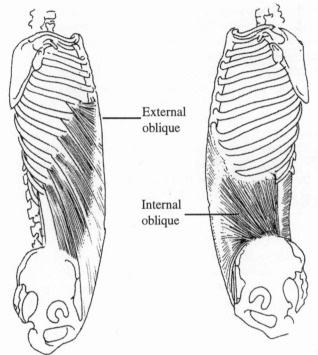

External oblique

Internal oblique

Figure 2.6
External and Internal Oblique Muscles
The broad muscles of expiration that pull down the thorax
and compress the viscera.

Ribs

There are twelve pairs of ribs. All are attached to vertebrae in the back. The first through the seventh pairs have cartilaginous attachments to the sternum, and the eighth to the tenth are attached to the seventh. The eleventh and twelfth pair of ribs are called floating. They have no attachment to the sternum at all. The expansion of the ribs increases the anterior/posterior dimension of the ribs as well as the lateral dimension.

The range of movement of individual pairs increases as they move away from their attachment to the sternum; that is, the lower pairs have more excursion than the upper pairs.

Lungs

The right and left lungs feature fissures that divide the overall structures into smaller lobes. The left lung has one horizontal fissure which divides it into two lobes. The right lung has one horizontal fissure and one oblique fissure that make for three lobes. The right lung is larger than the left owing to the relative position of the heart (see Figure 2.4). The lungs are soft, spongelike tissue made up of millions of tiny air sacks called alveoli (the leaves of the bronchial tree). The lungs are not hollow cavities. The alveoli pass gases in and out of the bloodstream to sustain life. Outbound gases traverse the alveoli, the tabules, bronchioles, bronchi, trachea, and finally the nose and mouth. The lungs are enclosed in a sac called the pleura. The pleura protects the lungs from friction against the wall of the thorax. It is formed of two layers that are separated by a serous fluid. The parietal pleura is the exterior layer and connects to the thorax wall, the mediastinal membrane, and the diaphragm. The shape of the lung closely follows the shape of the thorax because of this connection.

Diaphragmatic-Intercostal Breath Management

One of the confusing things about singing is the wide variety of terms used for the same or nearly the same thing. When talking about breath management, you may see these equivalent or nearly equivalent terms:

1. System of breathing for singing ~ breath management ~ breath support
2. Static moment between inhaling and exhaling when breathing muscles are balanced ~ point of suspension ~ moment of appoggio ~ point of balance
3. Moment *during* singing that feels like number two above ~ balanced support ~ appoggio ~ suspended tone
4. Process by which appropriate subglottal pressure, efficient fold vibration, and resonance are combined ~ connection ~ hookup ~ appoggio.

To add to the confusion, Italians can also refer to appoggio as the place where maximum tension or sensation is felt. There can be appoggio of the abdomen, the chest, the teeth, and so on. In order to avoid further confusion, let us describe a system of breathing for singing that uses only one term from the list above—breath management. In making this effort we realize that the practice of the system described may have amazing similarity to any or all the listed terms according to someone's interpretation of them.

Diaphragmatic-intercostal breath management is a system of breathing for singing that employs the following parallel activities during inspiration:

1. Downward movement of the diaphragm and the resulting displacement of the viscera
2. Raising of the sternum and increasing the circumference of the thorax

During exhalation the parallel activities include:

1. Tensing the muscles of the abdomen (which pushes the viscera up against the diaphragm) while—
2. Attempting to hold the position of the raised sternum and enlarged thorax

The basic activities of the diaphragmatic-intercostal system of breathing look simple. Unfortunately, because it is not exactly like breathing for living, all manner of extraneous muscle tensions will result in imbalances of the basic movements. Imbalance of the agonist (upward-moving diaphragm) and the antagonist (muscles holding the chest open) musculature can result in uneven airflows that will not support a tone of continuous quality. Clavicular breathing, exhibited by the movement of the shoulders; costal breathing, exhibited by the heaving chest; and purely diaphragmatic breathing, exhibited by protrusion of the belly, are examples of such imbalances. Tension in the neck can result in noisy breathing, which must be avoided. Taking too much breath, or crowding, can result in tension, which causes the air to be expelled too fast. Holding breath is a result of so much tension in the system that nothing can move.

Fine-tuning airflow from this system results in the optimal subglottal pressure for efficient vocal fold vibration. So-called *flow phonation* is the result of precise adjustments in air pressure, volume, and rate across perfectly adducted vocal folds and a resonator that is exactly in tune with the vibrator. The exact subglottal pressure is achieved through the agonist/antagonist action of the muscles of inspiration and expiration.

The following is a quick teach for diaphramatic-intercostal breath management. It is imperfect because it may require many directives to offset the tensions that arise when first attempting disciplined breathing. Exercises to reinforce the basic principles and some common directives follow.

Stand with feet apart about the width of the shoulders with one foot slightly ahead of the other. Pretend that a string is connected to the top of your head gently pulling you to your full height. Place one hand over the sternum, and the other over the upper abdomen. Take a breath as though you were filling the chest with air from the bottom up. Note that both hands go out as the chest expands. Exhale as though the air were coming from the bottom of the chest. Note that the lower hand goes in and the upper hand stays put. Don't allow the chest to collapse. Take the new breath by renewing the first. Only the lower hand moves this time.

Here are some exercises to reinforce diaphragmatic-intercostal breathing sensations.

1. Stand erect and lift your hands, arms straight, palms out, over your head as you inhale. Note the high position of your chest, the straightness of your back, and the lift you feel out of the pelvis. Slowly exhale the breath as you let your arms descend, making sure not to collapse the chest. Do the exercise over a few times, counting aloud as you exhale. Next, chant the numbers in an energetic monotone. Finally, on a comfortable pitch and vowel, sing for at least a count of ten slow beats as your arms descend.

2. Place your hand on the upper abdomen, about three inches below the sternum, and inhale and exhale slowly. Note the outward movement on inhalation and the inward motion on exhalation. Increase the speed of inhalation and exhalation until you can pant quite rapidly. This should remind you of what your dog does after a good run. Take care not to reverse the direction of the pant—it's always out for inhale, in for exhale.

3. Make a graphic representation of the expansion of

your ribcage during breathing by placing both hands, all fingers together and pointing outward, on each side of the lower ribs and apply a firm pressure. Note the pressure against your hands as you inhale. To check expansion in the other axis, place the thumb of one hand on the lower ribs in back while placing the palm of the other hand on your lower ribs in front. Put the finger tips of both hands together at the end of an exhalation. On inhalation, see how far you can make your fingertips on either hand separate. After some practice the fingertips should part at least an inch.

Respiration for singing can, and should be, practiced in places other than the practice room. You can practice breathing while you walk or sit with good posture. Just measure the inhalation and exhalation by counting the number of beats each takes. At first, inhalation and exhalation should be of about the same length. As you progress, try to make a complete, relaxed inhalation more and more quickly. Try to make your exhalation last as long as possible with airflow sufficient to support good tone. It does no good to win prizes for lengthy exhalation if the airflow rate is so small that it would not produce a singing tone.

Here are some common directives about breathing for singing:

- Breath through the nose when time allows and through the mouth when it does not.
- Sing in the position of breathing; breathe in the position of singing.
- A song begins with a complete breath that is renewed throughout the song.
- A catch breath is a normal breath taken more quickly.
- You must be as comfortable taking breath after a half phrase is sung as you are when a full phrase is sung.

MUSCLE	ORIGIN	INSERTION	ACTION
Abdom. diaphragm	Vertebral, costal, sternal	Central tendon	Domes flatten, pushing ribs out and viscera down
Pectoralis major	Top of the humerus	Fans out to clavicle, sternum and upper 6 ribs	Raises ribs
Pectoralis minor	Process of shoulder blade	Lower 5 ribs	Raises ribs
Levatores costarum	Spinal process of all vertebrae	First and second ribs below the point of origin	Raises ribs
Lattissimus dorsi	Top of humerus	Spinal process of lower 6 thoracic vertebra, crest of pelvis & lower 4 ribs	Raises ribs
Serratus posterior inferior	Attached to spine of vertebra 11&12 & 1st two lumbar vert.	Lower border of lower 3 or 4 ribs	Pulls down on the ribs to stabilize them against the contraction of diaphragm
Quadratus lumborum	Crest of pelvis	Twelfth rib	Depresses rib
External intercostal(11)	Lower border rib above	Upper border rib below	Raises ribs, holds pleura in
Internal intercostal(11)	Lower border rib above	Upper border rib below	Raises ribs, holds pleura in
Innermost intercostal (11)	Deep to internal intercostal	Upper border to next 2 or 3 ribs below	Depresses rib

Table 2.1
Muscles of Inspiration

MUSCLE	ORIGIN	INSERTION	ACTION
Rectus abdominus	Pubic arch	6th, 7th, 8th rib near the sternum	Compresses viscera via "bellies" which can contract the muscle in sections (sixpack belly)
Transverse abdominus	Barrel-like muscle; connects to lumbar fascia, inguinal ligament, crest of pelvis, lower 6 costal cartilages	Weaves into rectus abdom. & inferiorly to crest of pubic arch	Compresses viscera and squeezes thorax
External oblique	Outer surface of lower 8 ribs	Inguinal ligament & crest of pelvis	Compresses viscera and depresses thorax
Internal oblique	Lateral portion of inguinal ligament, crest of pelvis & lumbar fascia	Anterior fibers weave into rectus sheath & posterior fibers to low ribs	Depresses thorax
Transverse thoracis	Lower portion of sternum	2nd to 6th ribs	Depresses ribs

Note: A fascia is a sheet of connective tissue covering or binding together another structure.

Table 2.2
Muscles of Expiration

Phonation

Phonation is making a sound. The mechanism of phonation is the larynx. It is connected above by a common air and food passage called the pharynx and sits across the the passage to the lungs, the trachea (windpipe). Its primary function is not to aid communication, but to act as a protective valve at the top of the trachea. It closes to prevent food particles from entering the lungs. Its sensitivity is such that particles invisible to the naked eye will cause a powerful cough reflex when they pass through. This is what happens when food goes down the wrong pipe or you try to inhale dusty air. Taking a breath and closing the larynx provides enough intrathoracic pressure to stiffen the thorax for lifting. The stiffened torso when combined with abdominal compression aids defecation, urination, and childbirth.

The larynx is very mobile. If you put your finger lightly on the Adam's apple (anterior prominence of the thyroid cartilage) to mark its place, and look in a mirror, you can see the larynx rise when you swallow and descend when you take a deep breath. The larynx is suspended between connective tissues rather than being attached directly to bone, which is why its operation is rather complex.

Cartilages

The larynx is formed by three large cartilages and two smaller ones. Building from the bottom, they are the cricoid, thyroid, arytenoids, and epiglottis. The first two are made from hyaline, which can ossify with age. The ossification of cartilage combined with the thickening of lubricating fluids can change the flexibility of the voice.

The cricoid cartilage, sometimes called the signet ring cartilage, encircles the trachea and forms the base of the larynx. The ring is taller and wider at the back and has two pairs of facets (notches where other bones can connect). The top facets connect the arytenoid cartilages, and the lateral facets connect to the inferior cornu (horns) of the thyroid cartilage.

The thyroid cartilage, sometimes referred to as the shield cartilage, is made of two plates (laminae) that connect in the front by a different angle in men and women. The smaller angle in men produces the prominence we call the Adam's apple. The vocal folds are attached to the thyroid just behind the notch (Adam's apple), and the cartilage has a superior and inferior pair of cornu in the back. The upper cornu connects by ligament to the hyoid bone, and the lower rides in the cricoid facets.

The paired arytenoid cartilages are smaller than the others and shaped like pyramids with a front and back projection at their base called processes. The front process is called the vocal process because it attaches to the vocal ligament, and the back process is called the muscular process because it attaches to the cricoarytenoid muscle. The arytenoid cartilages sit in the top facets of the cricoid. Because of their muscular attachment and the shape of the facets, they are capable of gliding and rotation which can bring the vocal processes together and allow them to move front to back. When the vocal processes are pulled together the folds are said to adduct, and when they move apart they are said to abduct.

The epiglottis is an elastic, leaf-shaped cartilage that attaches to the inner wall of the thyroid just below the notch. Superiorly, it attaches to the base of the tongue and to the hyoid bone by the hyoepiglottic ligament. The epiglottis forms the anterior wall of a chamber. When you swallow, the epiglottis folds over the chamber and collapses it as the vocal folds close, thereby sealing off the trachea. The chamber made by the epiglottis is an important one for resonance of the voice. In fiber optic studies the epiglottis can be seen to stop at various phases of opening and closing. The changing dimension of the chamber helps to to form different vowel sounds.

The hyoid is a horseshoe-shaped bone that is not a part of the larynx but is very important to it. Its superior attachment is to the tongue and floor of the mouth, which are in turn connected to the jaw and skull. It suspends the larynx by way of attachment to the thyroid through the thyrohyoid membrane and the superior cornu of the thyroid. It is steadied by thin strap muscles that arise from the vertebrae and clavicle below.

An easy way to remember these structures is to think of their shapes from bottom to top: ring-shield-pyramids-leaf-horseshoe. A mnemonic would be: the valuable ring is protected by the shield and the pyramids leafed over by a horseshoe.

Intrinsic Muscles

The muscles of the larynx can be thought of as systems of twos. There are two classifications of muscles. The intrinsic muscles connect the cartilages of the larynx, and the extrinsic muscles connect the larynx to surrounding structures. The muscles are paired (sets of two) with one on each side of the midline of the larynx. An example would be the thyroarytenoids. The muscles function by twos. One muscle pulls in

one direction (agonist) and its partner pulls in the other direction
(antagonist). The intrinsic muscles control two basic conditions of the
the folds: thickness and proximity. The muscles lengthen and stretch

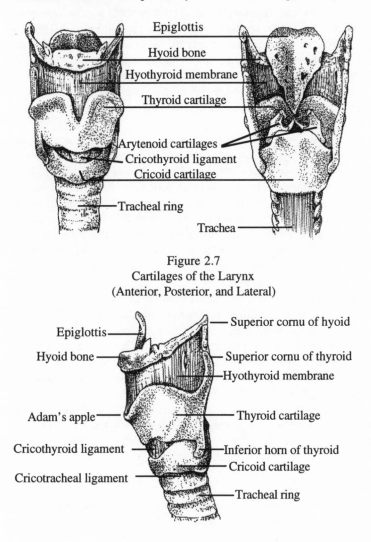

Figure 2.7
Cartilages of the Larynx
(Anterior, Posterior, and Lateral)

the folds for light registration and high pitches, and shorten and thicken the folds for heavy registration and lower pitches. The folds can be adducted for singing and speaking, and abducted for breathing.

The intrinsic muscles that abduct the vocal folds are the posterior cricoarytenoids. They pull the muscular processes of the arytenoids toward them, rotating the vocal processes away from the midline of the larynx. They are functioning with every breath we take and are working in opposition to the vocalis muscle and the cricothyroids.

The muscles responsible for adducting the vocal folds are the lateral cricoarytenoids and the interarytenoids. The lateral cricoarytenoids rotate the vocal processes of the arytenoids toward each other (bringing the vocal folds along with them). The interarytenoids pull the pyramids together closing up the posterior end of the folds. The glottal chink that may result from the incomplete action of the interarytenoids is the source of breathiness heard so often in immature voices.

The cricothyroids stretch the vocal folds by pulling the thyroid cartilage forward and tilting the cricoid cartilage backward.

The vocalis muscle, or the internal thyroarytenoids, forms the main body of the vocal fold. It is divided into two bundles. The vocalis is thought to be used for adjusting the tension of the medial fibers, and the muscularis for quick shortening of the folds.

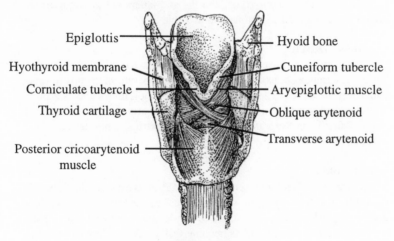

Figure 2.8
Intrinsic Muscles of the Larynx
(Posterior View)

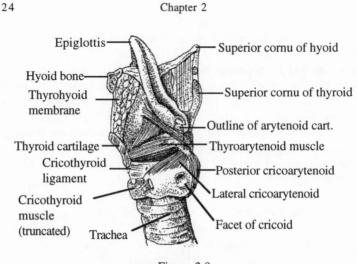

Figure 2.9
Intrinsic Muscles of the Larynx
(Lateral View)

A way to remember the intrinsic muscles is to associate them in broad terms with what they do. The adductors are the lateral and interarytenoids. The abductors are the posterior cricoarytenoids. The fold stretchers are the cricothyroids, and the shorteners are the thyroarytenoids. The muscles are summarized in Table 2.3.

Extrinsic Muscles

The extrinsic muscles connect the larynx to outside structures. Their importance stems from their ability to operate in groups to raise and lower the larynx. Their exact operation as individuals and as groups is always subject to some interpretation. The muscles are subdivided into infrahyoid and suprahyoid groups. The extrinsic muscles are summarized in Table 2.4.

Vocal Folds

There are actually two sets of vocal folds, the true and the false vocal folds. The false folds are sometimes called vestibular because they are the upper boundary of a small vestibule above the true folds. Both sets of folds can vibrate. It has become fashion for some wind players to play triple stops: one note with the instrument, one note from the true fold, and one very soft note from the false folds. Occasionally you

MUSCLE	ORIGIN	INSERTION	ACTION
Posterior crico-arytenoids(2)	Posterior surface of cricoid	Muscular process of arytenoid cartilage	Primary abductor of vocal folds
Lateral crico-arytenoids(2)	Superior borders of cricoid arch	Muscular process of arytenoids	Rotates arytenoids bringing vocal processes together
Interarytenoids (transverse & oblique)	Posterior surface of outer borders of arytenoids	Apex (oblique) and outer (transverse) border of arytenoids	Draws tips and bodies of arytenoids together to close glottis
Cricothyroids(2)	Front arch of the cricoid	Lower lamina and inferior cornu of thyroid	Pulls thyroid cartilage forward and tilts cricoid backward
Thyroarytenoids Vocalis Thyromuscularis	Angle of thyroid cartilage Angle of thyroid cartilage	Arytenoid cartilage Arytenoid cartilage	Fine adj. of medial fibers Quick shortening of folds

Table 2.3
Intrinsic Muscles of the Larynx

MUSCLE	ORIGIN	INSERTION	ACTION
INFRAHYOIDS			
Sternohyoids(2)	Posterior of sternum	Hyoid bone	Pulls hyoid to sternum & consequently lowers larynx
Sternothyroids (2)	Posterior of sternum	Side of thyroid	Draws thyroid down directly depressing larynx
Thyroid muscles(2)	Side of thyroid	Front of hyoid bone	Elevates larynx and/or depresses hyoid
Omohyoids(2)	Top of scapula	Inferior border of hyoid	Depresses and pulls hyoid backward
SUPRAHYOIDS			
Stylohyoid	Temporal bone	Hyoid bone	Elevates hyoid and larynx
Anterior digastric Posterior digastric	Fore part of lower jaw & hyoid bone	Mastoid process Mastoid process	Retracts mandible Elevates hyoid
Geniohyoid, hyoglossus & mylohyoid	Tongue	Hyoid bone	Tongue forward: hyoid elevates Tongue down: hyoid descends

Table 2.4
Extrinsic Muscles of the Larynx

will hear a singer who can sing in harmony with him- or herself, but the note from the false folds is very soft. It requires a tense contortion of the singing mechanism to bring the false folds into phonation and is best avoided by the serious singer.

The true folds are made up of the vocalis muscle, the vocal processes of the arytenoid cartilages, and the vocal ligament. The vocal ligament forms the top border of a tough elastic sheath that arises from the upper surface of the cricoid. When the folds are vibrating the elastic sheath (conus elasticus) makes a sort of upside-down funnel from the cricoid to the folds. The false folds supply most of the mucous that lubricates the true folds as they vibrate. The folds generate friction when they vibrate and the lubrication helps carry heat away.

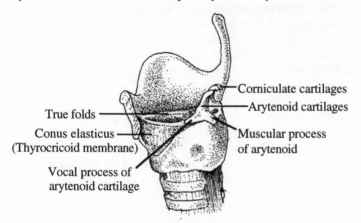

True folds
Conus elasticus
(Thyrocricoid membrane)
Vocal process of
arytenoid cartilage

Corniculate cartilages
Arytenoid cartilages
Muscular process
of arytenoid

Figure 2.10
Cutaway View of the Larynx

Above the ventricular folds are two structures that can help close off the trachea. The quadrangular membrane and the aryepiglottic folds form the cavity above the true folds over which the epiglottis closes in swallowing.

The vocal fold structure has been the object of research in the last twenty years (Hirano, Kurita, & Nakashima, 1981; Hirano & Sato, 1993). The evolving system of nomenclature for the layers of the folds is up to five. The outermost layer is 0.05 to 0.1 millimeters thick and is made of squamous epithelium (similar to the lining of your cheek). The next layer is called the lamina propria and has three layers within it. The superficial layer is about 0.5 millimeters thick and is composed of elastin and interstitial fluids (similar to jello). This layer is also known as Reineke's space. Reineke's edema is a condition associated with vocal hyperfunction and systemic disease such as hypothyroidism and occurs in Reineke's space. The intermediate layer is composed of the same materials but has some collagen added to it (similar to cold jello). The last deep layer is primarily collagen (similar to very cold jello). The last two layers combined total one to two millimeters in thickness, the whole lamina propria being less than three millimeters thick. The fifth layer is the thyroarytenoid muscle itself and is about seven to eight millimeters thick.

The tissue of the folds changes through its length. In general, the ends where the folds attach to larger cartilages is firmer than the medial section. A mass of collagenous fibers called the anterior commissure tendon is located at the anterior end of the folds. The posterior end of the folds is less well defined. Many sources define it as the junction with the vocal processes of the arytenoid.

Subglottal Pressure

The vocal folds respond to changes in subglottal pressure (pressure created by expired air against the closed folds). Subglottal pressure can vary from two to fifty centimeters H_2O in a singer, which is much less air pressure than wind players apply to the lips. Mechanoreceptors (nerves that sense motility) in the subglottic mucosa are sensitive to air pressure changes and can influence a reflex reaction by the intrinsic muscles of the larynx (Abo-El-Enene, 1967). This is why sudden bursts of expired air are so difficult to control. Maintaining a constant subglottal air pressure requires a balanced and coordinated effort between the muscles of inspiration and expiration. For example, the intercostals have mechanoreceptors that can help them make fine adjustments to air pressure.

Airflow is the companion to subglottal pressure. Airflow in singing can vary between 100 and 200 milliliters per second. When the folds are tightly adducted the rate of airflow decreases. The inverse is also true: when the folds are loosely adducted airflow rates increase. At very low pitches laryngeal control dominates airflow in changes of intensity. At high pitches airflow dominates laryngeal control (Isshiki, 1965).

Onset

Phonation is an uncomplicated act done naturally by everyone. For the singer, this uncomplicated act takes on the character of a very complicated act because it involves a very precise beginning to the tone and a very precise release. The appoggio is most often referred to by Italian teachers as the major technique for connecting breath to tone. *Appoggiarsi a* means "to lean upon" and involves the whole gestalt of taking breath, suspending it for a moment, phonating and resonating.

FRONT

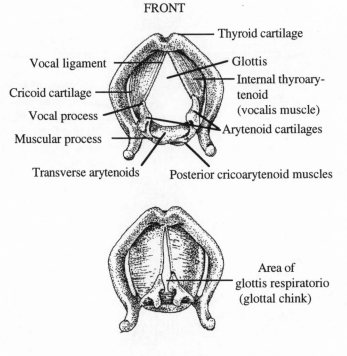

Vocal ligament
Cricoid cartilage
Vocal process
Muscular process
Transverse arytenoids

Thyroid cartilage
Glottis
Internal thyroary-
tenoid
(vocalis muscle)
Arytenoid cartilages
Posterior cricoarytenoid muscles

Area of
glottis respiratorio
(glottal chink)

Figure 2.11
Looking Down on the Folds (Open and Approximated)

Singers are sometimes implored to "attack" the tone. This generally results in a tone that is pinched at its onset and seldom resonant. In addition to the objectionable sound, this onset is created by a glottal stroke. In the glottal stroke the vocal folds strike each other forcibly,

Figure 2.12
Laryngeal Vibration

Single phase of laryn-
geal vibration as seen
in cross section of the
folds and from above.
Dotted lines indicate
motion.

resulting in swelling of the folds and potentially worse physical conse-quences. The ideal onset coordinates breath and tone production precise-ly for a soft beginning to the tone. Begin tone with an audible "h" until you can substitute a silent "h" at onset. Likewise, releases can be made hard and soft. The soft, balanced re-lease is most easily attained by thinking of continuing the airflow after the tone stops. Remember that tone ceases when airflow is no longer adequate to cause the folds to produce the desired pitch. The hard release, which is often heard among opera singers, is a vocal effect and not in-tended for habitual use. It is obtained by a quick flex of the diaphragm at the release and feels very much like a grunt.

Vibrato

Vibrato is a concept looked upon with some skepticism by the be-ginning singer, because pop singers, rock singers, and country and western singers don't use vibrato at all. Jazz singers and some standards singers (music from the 1920s to 1950s) use it very selectively, usually at the ends of notes. The aesthetic of classical singers is to use vibrato almost all the time. Exceptions are made for special effects like feigned voice or falsetto singing. Vibrato was defined by Seashore (1936) as a "pulsation of pitch usually accompanied with synchronous pulsations of loudness and timbre, of such extent and rate as to give a pleasing flexibility, tenderness and richness to the tone." The pulsation of pitch mentioned is usually a quarter tone above and below the target pitch. The average rate of vibrato is from 4.5 to 6.5 hertz, although not all authorities agree on this matter (Titze, 1994, 291 and Miller, 1986, 182). Singers who have a wider extent of pitch and slower rate of vibra-to are described as having a wobble. Singers with narrower extent and faster rate are said to have a bleat. Vibrato extent and frequency increase naturally with ascending pitch. Vibrato extent decreases when negotiat-ing runs so that pitch is more precise.

Singing teachers have been speculating about the physiological cause of vibrato for a very long time. Earlier in the century it was the-orized that vibrato was an aerodynamic event. Fluoroscopic pictures showed singers whose diaphragms were moving in synchrony with their vibrato rate. It was thought that the larynx was responding to that une-ven airflow by changing pitch. Higher air pressure made pitch ascend and lower air pressure made pitch descend around a mean pitch deter-mined by the tension of the folds. The same kind of logic was used by those who believed vibrato was produced by the movement of the jaw or larynx. All of those behaviors can be observed in singers, although vibrato is heard from fine singers with none of those behaviors as well. The current theories credit neurological pulses for changing the tension on the vocal folds and creating the vibrato. The analogy is made that the voice is vibrating at about the same speed as the muscle tremors you experience while lifting a too heavy weight. Here is one of the theories put forth:

> The origin of vocal *vibrato* is not well understood, but some evidence is beginning to show that vocal *vibrato* may be a stabilized physiologic tremor in the laryngeal muscles (Ramig & Shipp, 1987). It is conceivable, though speculative at this point, that a natural vocal *vibrato* can be cultivated from a 4 to 6-herz physiologic tremor in the cricothyroid and thyroarytenoid muscles. (Titze, 1994, 289)

Irregular vibrato rates, or no vibrato at all, are the result of imbalances between subglottic pressure, the intrinsic musculature of the larynx, and the external supportive musculature of the neck. Generally, wobble is the result of poor breath management. Inadequate subglottal pressure allows the folds to slacken. The singer usually has a timbral ideal that is too dark. Exercises that balance support (onset and agility) and a brighter ideal tone will solve the problem. Tremolo is the flip side of wobble. Tremolo is usually the result of too much subglottic pressure. Singers with tremolo are sometimes excitable and volatile. Learning real relaxation techniques, pulling some of the pressure off the vocal folds, and adopting a new tonal ideal (without tremolo) will help to cure the problem.

The most likely problem for a beginning singer is not tremolo or wobble, but no vibrato at all. Many times vibrato is avoided because the culture we live in does not offer it as an ideal. Accepting vibrato as a natural phenomenon that extends the expressive possibilities of the voice is an important step allowing vibrato to happen. Vibrato can be approached by imitating an opera singer or the kind of excited shaking of the voice that you hear in evangelical preachers on television. Breath management techniques that rely on slight, almost imperceptible pulses of the diaphragm are successful. Careful use of the onset exercises and pulsated drill in Chapter 7 can be helpful. Sometimes visualizing motion at a periodic rate, like a bouncing ball or a turning wheel (particularly if you imitate the motion with your hand), is helpful.

Vibrato requires balance in all areas of the singing system. A bouncing belly, a heaving chest, a waving larynx, or a tremulous jaw are steps in the wrong direction, even if considered a means to an end.

Resonation

To the general public, no facet of vocal technique so marks the difference between singers and non-singers as resonance. The ability to fill a room with sound, particularly a large room, should be one of many goals the student of singing desires to attain.

The quickest way for the student to attain resonance in the singing voice is to understand how the mechanism works. As stated earlier, air from the lungs is divided into puffs of air by the opening and closing of the vocal folds. The voice source thus produced is a complex spectrum of sound composed of a fundamental frequency (the pitch) and its overtones (integer multiples of the fundamental pitch). Because the spectrum of the glottal source is very wide, some overtones (and/or vowel formants) are enhanced in strength (resonated) and some are attenuated (filtered out) as they pass through the cavities of the vocal tract (pharynx, mouth, and sometimes nose). The result of the phenomenon of resonance is that the voice source, which sounded like the buzz made by a trumpeter's lips, sounds like the voice we speak and sing with as it leaves the mouth. The size and shape of the cavities and the surface characteristics of their walls create different areas of energy in the vocal spectrum that we interpret as vowels. Generally, two areas of energy, or formants, are needed for the ear to interpret the sound as a vowel.

Many pedagogues have put forth the analogy that the vocal tract is like a chain of connected resonators. Helmholtz resonators are made of brass and can be varied in the same parameters as their human counterparts. They have variable cavity size, variable length and width of neck, and variable orifice size. Each cavity, when a sound enters it, responds to its resonant frequency in the same way a soda bottle responds to only one frequency when you blow across the top of it. The physical laws that apply to the Helmholtz resonators are the same laws that apply to the vocal tract:

- The larger the cavity, the lower the frequency to which it will respond.
- The larger the orifice, the higher the frequency to

which it will respond.
- The longer the neck, the lower the frequency to which it will respond.
- The softer the cavity walls, the lower the frequency to which it will respond.

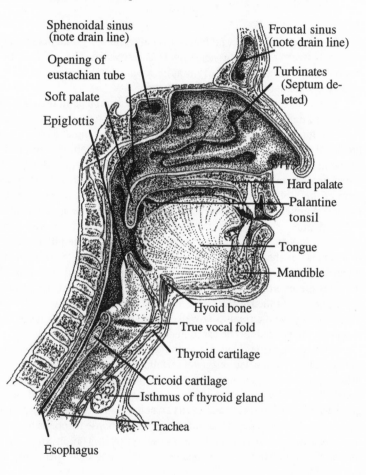

Sphenoidal sinus (note drain line)

Frontal sinus (note drain line)

Opening of eustachian tube

Turbinates (Septum deleted)

Soft palate

Epiglottis

Hard palate

Palantine tonsil

Tongue

Mandible

Hyoid bone

True vocal fold

Thyroid cartilage

Cricoid cartilage

Isthmus of thyroid gland

Trachea

Esophagus

Figure 2.13
The Human Resonating System

The pharynx, the mouth, and (when the nasal port is open) the nose, all contribute their own resonant pitches to the overall tone, which in turn forms the vowels and the overall timbre of the voice. A simple example of how this system works will make the theory clearer. A male singer as analyzed on a spectrogram has an area of energy (formant) at 300 hertz which is formed by the sound passing through the pharynx. The pharynx is connected to the back of the mouth, which responds to a frequency of 1950 hertz. Finally, the area at the front of the mouth, just in front of the tongue occlusion, responds to a frequency of 2,750 hertz. (See Figure 2.14) These three areas of energy or resonance, when applied to the overall sound spectrum, yield the vowel sound of [i]. By changing the shape of the resonators to respond to different frequencies, and consequently shifting the areas of energy in the spectrum, we create different vowels and vocal timbre. The dark bands of the spectrogram in Figure 2.15 correspond to the formants. Note how they change as the vowels [i,e,a,o,u] are sung. The area of energy between 2,500 and 4,000 hertz is usually defined as the singer's formant. It is this formant that gives the ring or carrying power to the voice. It is, incidentally, an area of the tonal spectrum that is not strong in most orchestral instruments. That is why a single resonant voice can usually be heard when accompanied by an orchestra.

Because the vocal tract operates on the same principles as the brass resonators, we can make some obvious assumptions about the voice. For example, all other factors being equal, enlarging the pharynx will give the tone a darker timbre. A larger cavity will respond to a lower frequency. Enlarging the mouth opening will give the tone a brighter timbre. A resonator with a larger orifice responds to higher frequencies.

Finding the correct configuration of the vocal tract to produce a given vowel sound is relatively easy in the middle of the voice. As pitch ascends, some modification of the vowel is necessary to prevent a shouty or screechy tone. Vowel modification, *copertura, aggiustamento,* vowel tuning, and formant tracking are some of the terms used to describe this process.

> The principle of vowel modification is that the initial vowel undergoes some migration as the scale ascends, by modifying toward a near neighbor. The laryngeal configuration changes for each vowel, and there should be corresponding change in the shape of the resonator tract. When the filtering aspects of the vocal tract are in tune with laryngeal configurations, the

vowel is properly "tracked." Vowel modification in the ascending scale permits vowel tracking and balancing of the formants (area of acoustic strength), thereby avoiding either "open" or heavily "covered" singing. (Miller, 1993, 41)

Vocal intensity is boosted dramatically when F_0 [fundamental frequency] is high and a harmonic coincides *exactly* with a formant. This is called *formant tuning*. It can be exploited in singing and theatre speech, in which fundamental frequencies can be so high that some of the formants may not be energized by the widely spaced harmonics (Acker, 1987; Raphael & Scherer, 1987). The problem of widely spaced harmonics is particularly acute for sopranos. A small mouth opening for the vowel [a] produces a mismatch between F_1 [first formant] (800 Hz) and F_0 [fundamental frequency] (1052 Hz, a female high C). By lowering the jaw (and perhaps raising the larynx slightly), F_1 can be increased to match F_0 to maximize their vocal intensity. (Titze, 1994, 231)

Perception and Placement

Young singers often confuse their aural perception of timbre with the physical sensation that the timbre creates. Many singers say they feel the [i] vowel at the bridge of the nose, the [u] vowel at the back of the head, and so on. Association of timbre with a place of production has led to the use of the term "placement." Since everyone has a different perception of timbre on different vowels, it is very difficult to teach students to sing by telling them to feel the resonance of the vowel in this place or that, since they may not feel it there no matter how well it is produced. The most efficient way to balance the resonators and find the most resonant position of the vowel is by auditor feedback. When the auditor recognizes the best sound the singer can make on that particular vowel, he or she can reinforce that perception to the singer. The singer can memorize what it felt like and then reproduce it at a later date (ideally at next week's lesson). Singers cannot perform this service for themselves because bone conduction, the air conduction of sound through the eustachian tube, and the air conduction of sound as it exits the mouth arrive at the ear as vastly different stimuli. For example, as the pitch of the voice goes higher, the upper partials of the voice become more directional and less heard at the ear while bone conduction remains the same. The result is confusion. Generally, the better your voice sounds to you, the worse it sounds to us.

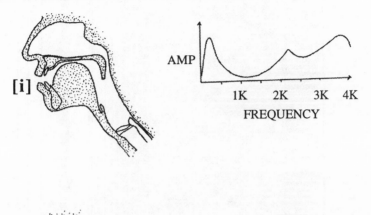

[i]

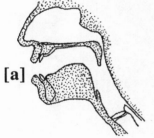

[a]

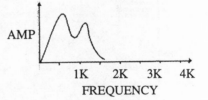

[u]

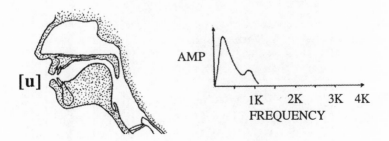

Figure 2.14
Position of Vocal Tract relative to Sound Spectrum in
the Vowels [i,a,u]

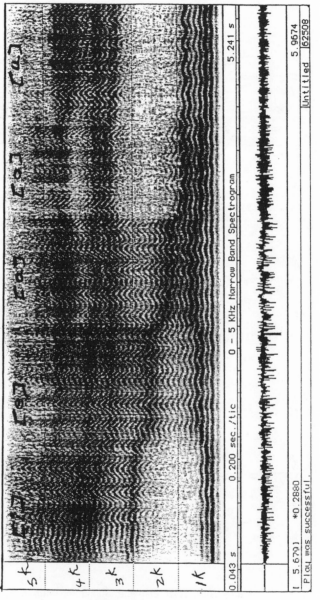

Figure 2.15 Sonogram

Gola Aperta

Gola aperta, or the open throat, is the backbone of resonant singing. The concept is implied in directives like "sing with space around
the vowel," "place the voice," and "open the tone." All of these directives have the same physical intent: to get the student to enlarge the
resonating system. This is accomplished by lowering the larynx and
raising the soft palate (increasing the vertical dimension of the pharynx)
and increasing the diameter of the pharynx. Imagery abounds in this area
of teaching. Students may hear the following:

1. Think of holding a pear in your mouth, big end at the
   back (pear-shaped tone?).
2. Try to sing through the same vocal position you have
   at the beginning of a yawn.
3. Yawn-sigh into the tone.
4. Try to recreate the same position for the tone that you
   have as you begin to gag or throwup.
5. Try to recreate the position of the throat when last
   someone surprised you by throwing a ball at your
   face.
6. Pretend you are across the street from a friend and you
   want to call to him or her without screaming In a
   very broad tone while waving so as to be seen at a
   distance call "Hey, hey!"
7. Inhale and sing through an [o].
8. Recreate the same position for singing as you had at
   the beginning of a breath.
9. Recreate the open feeling of the throat you have as
   you suck through a straw.
10. Imitate an opera singer.
11. Assume the throat position you might have if you
    wanted to smile, but could not let anyone see it (inner
    smile).
12. Recreate the position of the throat as you sniff the
    fragrance of a lovely rose.

Registration

When a young singer attempts to sing the whole of his or her vocal range, he or she will find areas of the voice that sound different. The

transition between those distinctive parts of the vocal range will often be marked by dramatic events that resemble a yodel. A vocal register is a series of notes in the vocal range that are produced by the same mechanism and have the same timbre. The abrupt transition between registers is generally called a break. The phenomenon of the break has a very complicated list of anatomical causes and interactions, but in simplest terms it results from inadequate coordination of airflow, laryngeal tension, and resonator configuration.

There are as many theories of registration as there are teachers of singing. Most theories differ on the length of the register, where the transition points should be, and what timbre a given register should be for a particular voice type in a particular singing style. This is one of the ways that individual teacher preference shapes the overall timbre of the student. For instance, one teacher might find it acceptable for a soprano singing a show tune to sing an [a] forte on B4 in chest. Another would demand that the art song rules be obeyed at all times and require her to sing it in head register.

The Italian school defines two registration events in all voices: the *primo* and *secondo passaggio*. There may be, and in fact usually are, several registers intervening between the main transitions. The main registers carry names associated with where the singer feels they are produced. Chest register (*voce di petto*) is the lowest register and is found in men's and women's voices. The next register, also in men's and women's voices, is head register (*voce di testa*). The highest register in the male voice is called *falsetto* because it sounds like a male falsely sounding female. An additional register is noted in some women's voices and is called flageolet or whistle. Mariah Carey has made this register a highlight of pop music. The following chart lists some typical transition points. The range below the first transition is chest. The range between the transitions is mixed voice (*zona di passaggio*), and the register above secondo passaggio is head. They should not be regarded as rules, all voices are different.

VOICE TYPE	PRIMO PASSAGGIO	SECONDO PASSAGGIO
Bass	A3	D4
Baritone	B flat3	E flat4
Tenor	D4	G4
Mezzo	F4	F5
Soprano	E flat4	F sharp5

The goal of all students of singing is to blend the registers together in such a way as to make the voice sound smooth and seamless. Some popular singers exploit obvious differences in register for effect or because they are not capable of smooth transitions. Female pop singers often make the transition to head voice very obvious. Male singers often flip into falsetto for effect. The serious singer should realize that good quality singing does not favor this aesthetic.

Many maxims for register blending exist in singing. Most are based upon concepts of vowel shaping and breath flow. The way to avoid a break in the voice is to increase air-flow and/or adductory pressure (the force that brings the folds together). Directives such as "support through the break," "add more air as you go up," and "add more air as you descend" all have their roots in this concept. While they often work, they are more useful for stretching a few extra notes from one register than they are for actually blending registers.

A mental concept which stresses the smooth and equalized range of the whole voice is more likely to pull the voice into line. Consider a technique that asks the voice to have no registers or breaks at all. To accomplish that task the following concepts will be helpful:

1. Observe the vowel migrations in Figure 2.16.
2. Think of the closed vowels opening as you ascend and the open vowels closing as you descend.
3. In scales, practice migrating your best vowel ([u or o]) across the break at different dynamic levels. When those are mastered go on to other vowels.
4. Try to allow as little change as possible in airflow volume and rate as you go through the passaggio. A marked change in vibrato is a clue to an imbalance in airflow and adductory force.
5. Practice crescendo and decrescendo on those tones that feel most likely to break.
6. Listen to good singers handle the break.
7. Practice the register-blending vocalises in this book.
8. Do not allow yourself to become frustrated. Pavarotti said it took ten years for him to smooth his way into top voice.

Articulation

Nothing is so important to the singer as being understood. A singer who is unable to effectively articulate the text relegates himself to life as an instrumentalist. Articulation, as it refers to text, is the relative position of the tongue, lips, jaw and hard palate as the phoneme is sung.

Pronunciation is the selection of the correct phoneme and its stress for a given pitch, duration, and intensity of tone. While this selection is rather easy in the middle range of the voice, it becomes a more complex issue as we ascend in range. Formant tracking or vowel modification (aggiustamento) is practiced by singers to give the aural impression of the correct vowel sound for intelligibility of text, even though the singer is producing a completely different vowel. This system of substituting vowels at various pitch and dynamic levels is a very old technique and is based on the fact that the ear accepts a wide variety of vowel timbres as intelligible. It is this fact that makes us able to understand baby talk, the accents of non-native speakers of English, and dialectal differences found in the United States.

Figure 2.16 is a vowel migration chart. It attempts to show the singer what vowels are readily available at a specific pitch and dynamic level for his or her specific voice type. To find what vowels are available on a specific note, find your voice type and place the note on the staff. If the note is below the primo passaggio (the lowest note written on the staff), all the vowels appearing in the square, upright ellipse, and flattened ellipse in the chart above are available. If the note is in between the two notes on the staff, the vowels in the square and flattened ellipse are available. If the note is above the high note on the staff, then only variations of [ʌ], the flattened ellipse, are available. Keep in mind that differences occur among individual voices. It might be possible for a truly lyric tenor to sing an [i] on F above middle C even though the chart says that vowel is not available in that pitch range. The chart admits the fact that the natural tendency during crescendo is to open the vowel sound with the increasing tone. It is advisable, however; to try to retain the original vowel sound in crescendo for greater textual intelligibility.

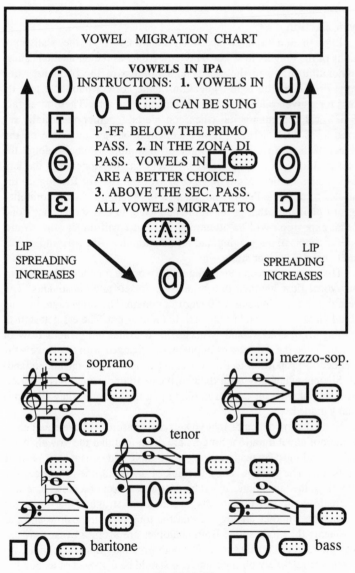

Figure 2.16
Vowel Migrations

Lyric Diction

Lyric diction has three facets. Articulation refers to the relative positions of the tongue, lips, jaw, and hard palate as the phoneme is sung. Enunciation refers to the clarity and fullness of the phonemes one sings. Pronunciation is the selection of the correct phoneme and its stress for a given pitch, duration, and intensity of tone. These three facets of vocal communication when considered together are usually referred to as lyric diction. Many excellent books are available on the subject of diction for singers. Some of them note in precise detail the exact position of the articulators for every single phoneme in the language being studied. Many have copious exercises for firming up the muscles of the articulators and practice for singing difficult combinations of phonemes that occur in the language. In this short space none of that exposition will be attempted. Instead I will direct you toward some concepts about singing and articulation that you will find immediately helpful to your study.

The average speech rate is about 250 words a minute with a continuous vocal flow blended into numerous vowels and consonants. The average word rate in song is 50 words a minute. The slower rate in song should yield a more intelligible text, but it does not. The ear determines meaning from context and is accustomed to the more rapid flow of speech. When the duration of phonemes is changed with the vowels far extended in proportion to the consonants, the result is misunderstanding. Singers eventually train their own ears to understand lyric diction and then make the mistake of thinking that the audience they sing to is equally trained.

Lyric diction demands that vowels and consonants have equal energy, but not equal duration. Singers are often told that the vowels carry the tone and must be made as long as possible and consonants as short as possible. The student is told to think of the vocal line as a stream of water from the faucet interrupted by the quick stroke of a knife. The water stream composes the vowels and the brief stroke of the knife the consonants. Another analogy is that the tone is a clothesline and the consonants the clothespins. Both analogies are useful in that they express the idea of constant tone, but both give the impression that consonants are relatively unimportant and should be disposed of as quickly as possible. This is an error. Uttering consonants quickly gives an ideal flow of connected pitch, but it always yields a barely intelligible text. Consonants should receive the same energy as vowels and a duration which can make them understandable to the untutored ear.

A common problem among young singers is "chewing vowels." The opening and closing of the jaw *during* the vowel produces the diphthonging that is easily recognized in country and western singing and the southern drawl. Holding the articulators, particularly the jaw, steady during the vowel will eliminate this problem. Contrast the first and second example of the sung text "O say can you sing" found below. Choir teachers have often conveyed this concept of prolonging the vowels over the whole value of the note by telling their singers to mentally repronounce vowels on succeeding beats.

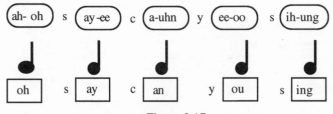

Figure 2.17
Singing Vowels without Added Diphthongs.

Vocal line is a concept bandied about by singers all the time, and it is usually misconstrued. Vocal line has three facets. The first facet involves connecting tone from note to note, regardless of the width of interval. The best note-to-note connection can be obtained from narrow-interval melodies sung on a single vowel. More technique is required to connect wide-range melodies with intervening consonants. Final consonants must always be tightly attached to succeeding vowels and consonants. (The Waring system of tone syllables was one of the first graphic representations of this concept.) Consonants come before the beat, and vowels on the beat. Releases, particularly consonants, need to be rhythmic and carefully timed to provide time for adequate breath before the next phrase. When possible, consonants should be voiced. The second facet of vocal line is connection of timbres. It is necessary to equalize the timbre of succeeding vowels in a vocal line. An extremely bright [i] vowel sung next to an extremely dark [u] vowel will be jarring to the ear. Both vowels need to be sung in the context of the whole line. The third facet of vocal line is dynamic connection. A very loud tone next to a very soft one will cause the soft one to be inaudible. The ear does not adjust to dynamic change rapidly enough to make both tones audible. I think this is one of the reasons that subtle dynamic shifts are such a common interpretive tool.

A high quality tape recorder can be extremely useful for assessing progress toward good vocal line and textual intelligibility. The student should remember that we all become accustomed to our own errors very quickly, and that fresh ears are often needed to evaluate a recording.

Chapter 3

For the Performer

Vocal Hygiene

Vocal health, or hygiene, has received lots of comment from modern pedagogues as singers become more sophisticated. Gone is the day when a singer could smoke, drink alcohol, go to sleep with the help of pills, and pop out of bed to sing a recording date the next morning (although I have heard of similar circumstances prevailing in the lives of rock musicians!).

Problems with the voice may be organic or functional. The majority of the pathologies common to singers are the result of singing with acute laryngitis (red, swollen folds) or some lesser, but chronic irritation. Here is a list of the most common pathologies:

1. *Laryngitis.* Edema and reddening of the larynx. May come as a result of many health factors but is most often a result of inhaling contaminants (cigarette smoke, fumes), allergy (dust, pollen, mold, perfumes), ingestion of toxins (alcohol), hyperfunction (too loud, too high, too long), and upper respiratory infections.
2. *Reineke's edema.* Edema in Reineke's space of the larynx. Female professional voice users seem to get this condition from either hormonal shifts or hyperfunction. It results in a very low speaking voice.

3. *Vocal-fold polyps*. Polyps on the folds that affect
   phonation. Generally caused by singing with an infection.
4. *Contact ulcers*. Ulcers in the region of the arytenoid
   cartilages. Caused by hyperfunction. May toughen
   and result in vocal nodules.
5. *Tumors*. Anywhere on the folds or attendant structures. They may be malignant or benign and most always have to be treated with surgery, chemotherapy,
   or radiation. Most prevalent among smokers.
6. *Recurrent laryngeal nerve paralysis*. The recurrent laryngeal nerve manipulates all the muscles of the larynx except for the cricothyroid. It runs from the brain
   all the way to the heart. (People having heart surgery
   should give this some thought.) Paralysis can occur
   during infection or surgery. Often the nerve regener-
   ates itself to restore vocal function.

Functional disorders always have their genesis in vocal abuse.
Adolescents going through puberty, high school cheerleaders and jocks,
and professional voice users all have a demonstrated form of vocal abuse
that may in time have a pathology to accompany it. Abuse results in
the following conditions.

1. *Laryngitis*. See above.
2. *Phonastenia*. Tired voice.
3. *Vocal nodules*. Callus-like swellings near the arytenoid cartilages that produce hissy phonation and loss
   of range. Result of hyperfunction (glottal attacks).
4. *Inappropriate mucosal lubrication*. Mucosa lubricates
   the folds during phonation and conditions the air
   coming through the nose. Problems result from simple hyperfunction after an upper respiratory infection,
   inadequate hydration, environmental factors, and hormonal imbalances.

All of these disorders can be treated by maintaining good health and
avoiding hyperfunction. Do not be surprised if your voice will not last
as long during singing as someone else's. Each of us, regardless of our
conditioning and health, shows varying amounts of vocal endurance.

Medication

Any medication that you take has the potential to affect your voice. The *Physician's Desk Reference* available at your local bookstore will give the classification, dosage, and contraindications of medicine you receive. In general, the following types of medicine should be avoided by singers if possible. Remember that good health with a medication is always preferable to bad health without it.

- *Antihistamines and decongestants.* Dry the throat and make it impossible to sing for any period of time. Can raise blood pressure. If these medications are prescribed for chronic allergy, remember to hydrate and avoid diuretics like alcohol and caffeine.
- *High-dosage birth control pills.* Can cause thickening of the vocal folds. These are less commonly prescribed now but are sometimes given to halt endometriosis.
- *Beta or calcium blockers.* Usually given for migraine or hypertension, they should not be used to control stage fright. Always cause dry mouth.
- *Mood alterers, tranquilizers, and sleeping pills.* Performers usually enjoy the edge needed to get through a performance. Those who need some kind of alteration usually require professional psychological help.

Treating Colds and Hoarseness

The singing teacher is probably asked almost as often as a physician how to treat an upper respiratory infection. Every cold takes a different course with different individuals. Usually a student will be symptom free in two weeks with no special medication or bedrest at all. He or she may be able to sing lightly all through this period, regardless of symptomatology. He or she may develop hoarseness as a result of coughing, laryngitis, or a secondary sinus infection. The secondary infection is usually cured by a round of antibiotics. Hard, prolonged coughing should be treated with an expectorant and cough suppressant like Robitussin DM. Hard coughing always results in damage to the folds, which will take more than two weeks' recovery time. Severe cases of laryngitis usually require intervention in the form of antibiotics and a corticosteriod. In general, avoid poor health conditions that lower your immunity. If you do get a cold cancel your voice lesson (none of us wants your cold), take acetaminophen for the headache, rest, drink fruit juices, and sing and talk only if your voice is clear. If conditions worsen beyond the scope of your regular cold—*go to the doctor.* Here are the steps usually recommended for good vocal health:

1. STOP—smoking (includes secondhand smoke), drinking alcohol, vocally risky athletic ventures (power lifting and aerobics till you drop), and recreational drug use. (Some teachers might include possessive boyfriends and girlfriends in this list!)
2. EAT—a well-balanced diet packed with nutritional food low in fat and high in carbohydrates, proteins, vitamins, and minerals.
3. DRINK—64 ounces of water or water-based drinks a day.
4. GET—good daily exercise. Train no more than three days per week.
5. SLEEP—8 hours *at night!*
6. AVOID—too much singing, speaking, yelling, cheering, or working in a hostile environment that might cause hyperfunction. This includes not only an atmosphere with chemical or particulate pollution, but high background noise as well (Lombard Effect). Avoid caffeine and diuretics.
7. PURCHASE—a humidifier if you find yourself in a dry climate, which includes hot hotel rooms and airplanes. Attempt to keep the relative humidity at thirty to forty percent in your environment.

Warming Up

While I was teaching in Georgia my school had a famous horn teacher in for a clinic with some of our horn students. My wife and I were honored when he agreed to stay overnight at our house. At least we were honored until 7:00 the next morning, when the sound of his long tone exercises broke the silence of our sleep and continued for half an hour. When I mentioned at breakfast that we had enjoyed hearing his playing, he looked puzzled and then very embarrassed. His daily ritual of warm-ups had become so routine and automatic that he didn't even think about them anymore, and certainly never considered that anyone would hear them!

As a beginning singer your warm-up should never be thoughtless or routine. Your teacher, after having analyzed your vocal problems, will prescribe a very specific set of exercises aimed at improving your particular voice. They should be practiced daily, and for just the amount of time the teacher prescribes, usually less than a half hour. Exercises may be assigned from the Singer's Tool Kit in Chapter 7.

Occasionally your teacher will ask you to warm-up during your lesson so that he or she can see whether you are using the exercises correctly. Your warm-up routines will change over time as your technique increases. New exercises will be assigned for perfecting new techniques. The amount of time you spend warming up will probably decrease as you become a more expert singer. Although your peers may be practicing exercises much different from your own, don't warm-up on just anything you hear floating around the practice rooms. It may do you more harm than good.

Warm-ups for the voice, just like warm-ups for the athletic body, will be isometric, isotonic, and calisthenic.

It is commonly known that many singers' practice regimens contain an abundance of rote ascending scales and many types of isotonic, florid scale work. Exercise of the isometric type is not always an essential ingredient. Even so, there is general agreement in the singing world that there exists a close correlation between the sound vocal technique the old Italian masters taught and their heavy reliance on "isometric" exercises such as the messa di voce (a specific frequency or pitch that is begun with a crescendo, sustained at a forte dynamic level, and ended with a diminuendo). Isometric exercises differ from isotonic or calisthenic-type exercises in that they are based on single, maximum contractions of muscle groups in which the contraction is sustained for a period of several seconds without motion. In contrast, isokinetic or isotonic exercises allow the muscle to change length at a very slow rate, and calisthenic-type exercises are composed of numerous short muscle contractions. (Sabol, Lee, & Stemple, 1995)

It is important to remember that warm-ups always start in the easy middle range of the voice and proceed outward, that the singing needs to be of moderate loudness or less, and that technique expansion exercises occur after the voice is warmed up. The typical warm-up will follow a pattern like this.

Physical Warm-up

The warm-up needs to be light. Its goal is flexibility, not strength training. Stretches used in dance class, yoga, a jazz curl, windmilling the arms, or a few soft step aerobics will be fine. Here are some of the musical activites that will be found in a well-balanced warm-up.

1. Humming. Easy mouth-closed and mouth-open humming on short scales and arpeggii in the middle of the voice. Humming exercises eventually open to the cardinal vowel sounds [i, e, a, o, u], mee-ah for example.
2. Onsets and offsets. (For examples, see breath exercises in Chapter 7)
3. Articulation. Brief articulation exercises which uncouple the movement of the lips, jaw and tongue from each other. On scales sing [bɛbɛ ...] while moving only the lips. Sing [lɑ lɑ ...] while moving only the tongue. Sing [jaja ...] while moving only the jaw (for other examples, see the articulation exercises in Chapter 7).
4. Agility. Begin with short scales and arpeggii on easy vowel sounds and progress to longer scales and arpeggii with more difficult vowels (for examples, see agility exercises in Chapter 7).
5. Range/passaggio. Exercises are based on descending scales and patterns through the passaggio. The basic exercise is a hoot or siren from the top down (for examples, see head voice and range exercises in Chapter 7).
6. Messa di voce. The final exercise of the warm-up is the classic crescendo-hold-diminuendo. For the beginning singer, this exercise will not have much dynamic range or length. It will be concentrated on notes easily produced with an eye toward regular vibrato. Research in singing is bringing new ideas to the classical concepts of warm-up, "support," and the value of soft singing. A recent study sought to link lower phonation threshold pressure to the effects of vocal warm-up (Elliot, Sundberg, & Gramming, 1995).

The idea was that increased blood flow to the folds would make them less viscous and therefore more easy to set in vibration. They would have a lower phonation threshold pressure. The warm-up effect varied considerably among the subjects. Apparently vocal fold viscosity was not a dominating factor for lowering phonation threshold pressure.

Vocal warm-ups are aimed at connecting breath to tone. In "Physiological Characteristics of the Singing Voice" (Griffin, Woo, Colton, Casper, & Brewer 1995), the researchers found through extensive objective and subjective measures that there was a great difference in "unsupported" and "supported" singing voice. The "supported" singing voice had the extra spectral characteristic of the singer's formant, higher sound pressure level, peak airflow, and subglottal pressure. Interestingly though, they found no significant difference in breathing activity between supported and unsupported singing. Singing teachers have long been divided on whether it is a good thing to practice very soft singing. The technique has been referred to as "singing on the soft." In two studies (Stemple, Lee, D'Amico, & Pickup, 1994; Sabol, Lee, & Stemple, 1995) it was shown that practicing a particular regimen of exercises at very soft volumes improved measures of flow rate, phonation volume, and maximum phonation times. That is, the exercises promoted glottal efficiency.

It is important to warm up and it is important to warm down. After a strenuous singing session, most singers will find it easier to warm up the next time if they warm down the voice. Stretching exercises including descending five tone and octave scales with light tone or humming will show where tension has accumulated during singing. Warming down will massage the substrates out of the vocalis muscle that might cause stiffening. The athletic corollary to a vocal warm-down is taking a liniment massage or jogging the victory lap.

How to Learn a Song

The craft of learning music often seems more difficult than it is because the discipline of learning has not been mastered. Often it seems easier to just bang out the notes of a song we like and thus begin a crude performance rather than take the time to go through all the steps needed to learn the piece. A true and thorough understanding of the song

cannot occur because some of the steps that would yield that understanding are left out of the learning routine. How often has a singer
with a beautiful voice and a wonderful song left you unmoved by his or
her lack of thoughtful preparation?

Here then are some—certainly not all—of the steps needed to learn
a song. In looking at this list you will understand that as singers become more adept musicians they spend less and less time on the beginning steps and more time on the artistic and interpretive steps. That is,
singing becomes an art instead of a craft.

1. Chant the melody on rhythm syllables.
2. Chant the melody on the words, if in a foreign language, write out the International Phonetic Alphabet
   transcription and place it beneath the words.
3. Sight-sing the melody (do not bang it out on the piano) using solfeggio or whatever method you have
   been taught. This is important because you can't keep
   up your sight-singing skills if you don't practice
   them! Check your sight-singing for errors on the piano.
4. Sing the melody with words.
5. Play the accompaniment. If your piano skills are inadequate for the task, reduce the accompaniment to
   chords and play it through. As before, your piano
   skills will not get any better without practice. As a
   last resort, have an accompanist record the accompaniment for you, knowing that you will lose all of
   your abilities to interpret (ritards, dynamics, and so
   on) if you listen to the tape too long.
6. Play the accompaniment as you sing through the
   song. As a last resort, play the tape as you sing
   through the song. Singers will want to get away from
   the piano once they have determined how everything
   fits together.
7. Library work. Know as much as you can about the
   poet and composer. Concentrate particularly on the
   milieu circa the composition. This includes details
   about their lives and analysis of their music. (Yes, I
   have handed in melodic and harmonic analyses of
   songs to my teacher before he would allow me to

sing them!) Listen to great performers sing works *other* than the one you are studying to learn about style and foreign language pronunciation.

8. Note the interpretive parameters of the song that the composer left for the performer (dramatic rests, accents, phrasings, dynamics, articulations) with an eye toward transforming the composer's intentions into your own.

9. Arrive at your personal interpretation of the piece based upon the completion of the preceding steps. This step sounds easy, but in fact it is the most important and most often neglected of all the steps. Trying to become the protagonist in the emotional minidrama that makes a good song is difficult. Experience in oral interpretation, reading the poem aloud to others, discussing and analyzing it with others, and projecting the song using the techniques of an actor is helpful.

10. Take the song to your lesson. Sing through it with accompaniment. Reshape the performance from feedback with the teacher and accompanist. Video-tape a performance and evaluate its effectiveness. Reevaluate with the teacher.

11. Memorize. If the preceding steps have been completed, this should be easy. If not, try the techniques listed in the section on memorization.

12. Practice performing with distractions to build concentration. A fellow student can lift your arms as you sing, talk to you, or make funny faces. Ask your pianist to intentionally try to throw you off by playing wrong notes and rhythms, deleting measures, or applying unexpected tempi. The test for whether your song is ready for performance is whether you can sing it to yourself in the mirror. If you have trouble looking at yourself in the mirror, think of the image as *it*. Become the teacher of *it* and try to improve the image's performance.

13. Schedule a live performance either in voice class or in a student recital. Evaluate feedback from peers critically. Revel in communicating with song!

How to Practice

Thoughtful, well-planned, patient practice that accomplishes specific goals is the key to learning to sing. Reaching goals, even small ones, makes us feel good and supplies the motivation needed to return to the practice room day after day. Great singers have found the joy obtained from learning something new in every day of their practice. The following regimen is recommended for singers at all levels.

1. THINK. Think about the goals and directives your teacher gave at the last lesson. Think about reasonable goals to attain in today's practice. Think about what techniques and/or music you will use to accomplish them. Think about how you will evaluate what you have done.

2. VOCALIZE. Generally, a little easy vocalization early in the day will increase the quality and quantity of your practice time. Vocalize to increase technique as well as to warm the voice. Ten or fifteen minutes of disciplined vocalization should be sufficient. Begin with long tones (onsets) at moderate dynamic levels in middle voice. Progress to slow scales and arpeggii, and end with agility and messa di voce exercises which encompass the full range and dynamics.

3. PRACTICE. Sing no more than thirty minutes at a sitting. Use rest periods to practice the accompaniment or memorize text. Avoid hyperfunction by practicing in a wide variety of ranges and dynamics. Use a hand mirror, full-length mirror, penlight and tape recorder for mechanical feedback as you practice.

4. INVITE PERSONAL FEEDBACK. Very often we do not hear what we really sound like. Invite a more experienced student to be your practice buddy and listen to your practice from time to time. Be aware that criticism should always be constructive and filtered through your own perceptions.

5. WORK ON ENSEMBLE. The delicate balance of interpretation and nuance in a performance comes from practice with an accompanist. Work toward art through interaction.

Building Relationships

A lot of what you learn about the being a singer and singing has to do with building relationships. Three kinds of relationships will be pivotal to your success. The first kind of relationship is teacher to student. Your relationship with your voice teacher is important because he or she is directly responsible for your growth as a singer. Relationships you build with other music teachers will be important too. The next important relationship will be with your accompanist or coach. That relationship will be important because it directly affects the way your performances in public are perceived. The last important kind of relationship to build is with your peers, your comrades in arms in the search for artistic expression. They will be important for your personal support and as added resources for your success in other areas.

Relationship with Your Teacher

The student–teacher relationship is one of the most complex relationships you will build. An experienced voice teacher is not only capable of supplying you with the technique you need to sing, but will be a mentor and motivate your growth as a musician as well. Because of the unique one-to-one dynamic of voice lessons, student and teacher come to understand each other's talents and goals fairly quickly. It is not unusual after some study for a student to regard his or her voice teacher as a second parent. It is also not unusual to hear voice teachers refer to their students in the same caring way they would talk about a member of their family. The dynamics of a family-like relationship between student and teacher are positive. The relationship promotes nurturing, efficient instruction, and a basis for mutually satisfying interaction.

In order for a family relationship to grow it must be nourished by meeting mutual expectations. Both the student and the teacher must honor the rules of respect, honesty, and commitment to work. The student shows commitment to work by practicing and taking care of any outside listening or writing assignments in a timely manner. The teacher is expected to be prepared for the student's lesson and provide a plan for the student's technical and musical growth. Both sides are obligated, and both sides are rewarded when the student excels.

One problem that pops up fairly often in the studio has to do with the way the student perceives feedback from the teacher. Many students are—or become through their voice training—very sensitive to criticism. This is because they have always sung for fun before and are now faced with having to sing in a competitive environment. There is nothing wrong with this state of affairs. It forces the student to look at singing as more than an attractive hobby, and it forces the teacher to regard every student's full potential for growth. The trouble occurs when either the student or the teacher holds some unrealized expectations that they do not make clear to each other.

The usual result of these unarticulated aspirations is either criticism or an unseasonable cooling of the teaching studio's atmosphere. In either case, both parties can overcome this problem by taking time to realize what they can and cannot reasonably expect from one another. The only way to be sure what two people actually want is for them to communicate. You should always feel free to talk earnestly with your voice teacher. In this way, hurt feelings and criticism flowing from both sides can be avoided.

Some rare students are not used to receiving any kind of criticism from anyone. Those students will find voice training very difficult. No one sings flawlessly, and the voice student is literally paying the voice teacher to criticize. The student should always remember that teachers try to deal with students in a professional manner. When a teacher speaks to you with criticism, it is of your voice alone. It is not a challenge to your self-worth.

Relationship with Your Accompanist or Coach

As a beginning student you may have accompanists of all types. In some schools your accompanist may be a piano student of your level taking accompanying for ensemble credit. Your accompanist could be a graduate candidate who accepts accompanying as part of his or her workload. Your accompanist could be a professional staff member who also accompanies instrumentalists and chamber groups. Your accompanist may be a coach who specializes in preparing singers for public performances in recital, opera, and musical theatre. The coach may be as well versed in languages and style as your voice teacher. All of these kinds of accompanists have something different to offer you by virtue of their experience and interest. They are an integral part of your musical family and have the same benefits and responsibilities that you extend to your teacher.

A few tips on working with your accompanist are in order:

    1. Try to have regular rehearsal times.

2. Listen when your accompanist corrects a musical error.
3. Work on your music with the understanding that the best ensemble is the result of musical give and take between performers. Interaction increases the performers' interest in each other and concomitantly the audience's interest in the performers.
4. Talk earnestly about tempo changes, balance, using rubato, pedaling, and anything else that affects your musical partnership.
5. If you supply copies for rehearsal, make sure all the music is on the page. Nothing is more annoying than finding a bass line missing at the bottom of a page.
6. Performances and most contests require the use of printed scores for the accompanist.
7. Spend some time with your accompanist playing "I'm the leader." The purpose of this game is to learn how to change a tempo once it is established, how to indicate the end of a fermata, how to signal that you want to start, and so on. It's helpful if both you and the accompanist get to be the leader sometimes. Following the accompanist occasionally can build the skill necessary to follow a strong-minded conductor!
8. There will be times when you are working with an unknown accompanist under performance pressure (contests, jury substitutes, auditions). In these cases *always* talk through the pieces with regard to tempi and phrasing before you go onstage. Once you are out there it is too late to talk about the cadenza!

Relationships with Your Peers

In a time when it seems there is a support group for everything, you will be glad to know there is one for singers. It's your fellow students. If you are learning to sing in a university setting, you will find that your peers are infinitely valuable in helping you thread your way through the system. Because everyone comes to school with different experiences, you will find buddies who are good at theory or music history or who play the piano. If you are studying privately, you will find encouragement and camaraderie from the other students in your studio. Voice classes in which everyone meets to sing for one another are an ideal time to get and give positive reinforcement to your peers. As they teach in business, the network can be a key to success.

When a Relationship Breaks Down

Occasionally there will be disruptions in the well-intended commerce of ideas between you and members of your musical family. Like all disagreements, ninety percent of the problems are directly related to failures to communicate adequately . Remember that you have not communicated unless the party you are speaking to can repeat what you have communicated and *understands* what you mean. If you are having a problem with your teacher, an accompanist, or a fellow student, the person to talk to is the person with whom you're having trouble. Problems are only made worse by talking to everybody else about your problem before you talk to the one person who has the immediate power to change things—the person with whom you are having trouble.

Sometimes students feel they would be better served by studying with someone else. In only a few cases is this actually better for the student in the long run. Implied in the students' desire to change is the idea that all of their vocal problems could be solved, if only they could change to another teacher. The process of vocal development is slow and is characterized by periods of great enlightenment followed by plateaus when it seems nothing is getting better. That is the nature of study. Changing teachers will not bypass all the plateaus!

One reason for not changing teachers has to do with the way other teachers will regard the change. Voice teachers look askance at "teacher hoppers." Although a teacher may be flattered that you want to change to his studio, his relationships with his fellow teachers are just as important as his relationship with you. You will be gone from a teacher's studio in a few years, but colleagues will be around for a long time. Most teachers are bound by ethics that will prevent them from taking you into the studio without the approval of your current teacher. When a teacher feels that a student would be better off studying with someone else, he or she will usually suggest the idea and help you find the right match. Remember, when you are having a problem with someone, he or she is the *first* person with whom to communicate!

Interpretation

The interpretation of a song brings to the understanding of an audience the message the composer desired to convey and the performer's personal response to it. It is the most intimate, interactive communication one can have with many persons at the same time.

Learning how to interpret a song or discovering the musical and verbal clues the composer left for you on a printed page is exciting. Imagine that the performer will bring the skills and knowledge gained through a lifetime of experience to bear on the intense performance of a two- or three-minute art song.

Stanislavski, the famous teacher of actors, called the art song a "microcosm of drama." Every song has a plot with a conflict and a resolution. Every poem has an intention that may supersede the obvious. Every recital has as many characters to portray as there are songs.

The way an artist arrives at a good re-creation is a highly individual experience. Careful analysis of how one artist gains insight might do the student no good at all, because it is an eclectic kind of study. Listed below are some of the considerations one should make in arriving at an interpretation.

1. Determine the mood of the piece and how it is defined in verbal and musical syntax.
2. Consider the ways in which that mood is best conveyed to an audience within the parameters of the performance medium. Use all resources available to realize that mood.
3. Study other disciplines pertaining to visionary performance. They include acting, dance (ballet), literature (particularly studies in verse), history (particularly European history), and the milieu of the composers.
4. Use the study of these peripheral areas as research to become the poet, the composer, or the speaker in a song.
5. Use the feedback given by your teacher and coach to form your interpretation. Always remember that the audience cares for your interpretation, not the aping of a bland or thoughtless student.
6. Before your first performance be able to successfully answer all of the questions below that apply to your re-creation of the song. The questions that could be asked about any great song are nearly endless, and it is discovering the meaningful answers to questions posed that builds an interpretation. The questions are

gleaned from *The Art of the Song Recital* (Emmons
& Sonntag, 1979, 127-128) and the work of Stanislavski. A mnemonic for recalling them is to group
them by the questions that need to be answered in a
newspaper article—who, what, where, when, and
why.

> *Who* is the speaker?
> Whom does he or she speak to?
> *What* is the speaker's subtext?
> What is the listener's subtext?
> What does the speaker perceive through all five
> senses?
> What does the listener perceive through all five
> senses?
> What is the speaker's physical and emotional state?
> What is the listener's physical and emotional state?
> What is the speaker's history?
> What is the speaker's history with the listener?
> What is the standing of their relationship?
> What happens when the text ends?
> What happens when the music ends?
> *Where* is the speaker?
> Where is the listener?
> *When* does the action of the song occur, and what effect
> does it have on the speaker and listener?
> *Why* am I singing instead of speaking? (What is my in-
> tention?)
> Why is the listener listening? (What is his or her in
> tention?)
> Why does my emotional state change?
> Why does the listener's emotional state change?
> Why does the listener respond?

We live in an environment that is flooded with salesmanship. Ads
on television every twelve minutes, print ads in magazines and newspa-
pers, and interpersonal contact with people who sell products have con-
vinced most of us that the only way to be successful is to "sell it." It is
in line with the heightened level of stimuli we experience and the
number of entertainment options available to the average person that we

must make our niche as a viable performance medium. Popular music has met this challenge by blitzes of publicity, literally becoming louder through amplification, concentrating on universal personal experiences (country and western), and selling sex as well as music (Madonna). With the tremendous resources available to the popular musicians, how will more traditional singers compete?

The viability of our art depends directly on the quality of the performances we give our audiences. It is our responsibility to interest them in an entertainment built upon diversity, nuance, and sophistication at a time in history when everything is louder, glitzier, and naughtier. This is not as impossible as it sounds. We have at our disposal a wide array of beautiful music expressing every facet of the human experience. We have the advantage of live, usually intimate performance venues, and a public that is increasingly hungry for entertainment that does not come through a speaker or a screen. We have the advantage of low overhead, and easy accessibility. But none of these items will work to our advantage if we cannot make the audience feel what we feel and see what we see.

Acting

Acting is the discipline that allows us to communicate to the audience what it is that we feel and see as we are singing. It is creating a reality for the audience and "living on the stage." Acting, in some form and to some degree, is omnipresent in interpersonal communications. It is the appliance salesman moving one more dishwasher out the door, it is the angry parent convincing a two-year-old why he must not walk into the street, and it is your professor telling you about the merits of singing German Lieder.

Since acting is something we all do naturally, why is it so difficult to bring what we feel to an audience in song? The barrier to our communication with the audience is not an unfamiliar musical vocabulary, syntax, or form. The barrier is not a foreign language, or a song or aria describing emotions and situations so far beyond our experience that we cannot relate to them. It is not a performing venue that does not provide enough stimulation for modern audiences. The barrier, assuming our singing is good, is poor acting.

Acting, as a discipline, falls into two major schools and one sub-discipline. The school of classical acting boasts the likes of John Gielgud and Laurence Olivier. It is most often found among actors interested in period works, embodies the study of fencing, acting with masks, mime, dialect, and production arts study. It is more often taught in its purest forms in western Europe. So-called method acting, or what the Europeans call the "American school," was actually transplanted from the teachings of Constantin Stanislavski at the Moscow Art Theatre in the 1920s, and 1930s. It is most often found among actors interested in realizing contemporary characters and is the most frequent choice of study for film actors. The great teachers of the method in the United States were Boleslavsky, Adler, Meisner, Kazan, Lewis, and Strasberg, all of whom wrote books. Several generations of actors have been influenced by the method. Among the names most prominent today are Barbra Streisand, Nick Nolte, Al Pacino, Meryl Streep, and Dustin Hoffman.

The subdiscipline of acting is the training of actor-singers. Stanislavski at one time aspired to be a singer and began training singers after his success with straight actors. Walter Felsenstein, Boris Goldovsky, and Wesley Balk have been the most influential agents for change in the acting style of singers in this country and have written and taught a great deal on the subject.

All of the teachers, whether of straight actors or actor-singers, espouse the doctrine of reality on the stage. Reality is arrived at through many different avenues, including classroom instruction, private lessons, even psychotherapy. No two teachers teach the same way, but most actor training in this country uses as its foundation the tenets of the method, even though the nomenclature may be changed to achieve distinction from what has gone before. Although it is not possible to learn to sing, act, or dance from a book, your understanding of the method and some of its derivatives will be enhanced by the following lexicon.

Action. Whatever happens on the stage must be for a purpose. An action springs from the emotional subtext of a situation, a motivation. It derives its power from the fact that it promotes the intention of the character. A gesture is never added just because there is time to fill, or because it may be interesting in another context. Gestures do not pantomime the words in "mickey mouse" fashion, but flow as natural reactions to emotion. In stylized singing situations (recital) the best rule is "less is more."

Affective memory (Strasberg, 1987, 69). Also called emotion memory (Stanislavski 1936, 158): inducing an emotional state by probing one's past experiences. For instance, remembering a time when someone near to you died will help you play a scene where you must show grief. The key to emotional memory is not to try and recapture the emotion, but to recreate the scene and events that spawned the emotion as carefully as possible. Emotion will flow in proportion to the strength of the detailed memory.

Animal exercises (Easty, 1981, 145). In order to increase the powers of observation, animals are imitated. Very often human characters exhibit animal characteristics. The physical persona Lee J. Cobb used in *Death of a Salesman* was an elephant. It best typified the aging, worn-out salesman lumbering around with heavy suitcases filled with samples.

Body language. (Rays in Stanislavski, 1936, 200) Communication through body postures and intensity of emotion. Beginning with Desmond Morris's *The Naked Ape*, science has codified much of our non-verbal communication.

Concentration of attention (Stanislavski, 1936, 72-94). All attention has to be focused on something or someone. For the singer in recital, that attention is generally an imaginary acting partner, usually sitting in the back of the hall. For an actor it can be a fellow player or even an object onstage. Actor-singers must be able to concentrate on many simultaneous events without being distracted into breaking character. A classic exercise in concentration is to ask a person to lift or move a piano while reciting a poem or doing arithmetic.

Cognitive dissonance (Term also used in educational theory). Studies have shown that emotions can be induced by indicating the emotion on the face. When patients were told to contort their facial muscles into postures of fear, they experienced the "fight or flight" reactions of racing heart, clammy palms, and so on. Emotions can work from the outside in as well as from the inside out. Action can induce emotion. This was Stanislavski's premise in the late 1930s. For the singer the implication may be that producing a tone that sounds like the emotion may induce the physical reactions which help relay the emotion to the audience.

If. Sometimes referred to as "the magic if." A singer uses imagination to project a different context for a song or aria. "If my character were in this particular situation (Stanislavski called it "given circumstance"), what would he do, what would he say?" If can construct new histories and new futures as well as new present contexts for the performer. Balk calls this concept a change in attitude and advocates changing the obvious attitude of a song or aria to explore new meanings. A happy aria could be sung as though you were really feeling sarcastic. Nuance of phrase can be exchanged for extravagance.

Improvisation. Situations are played out spontaneously, usually on a theme or germinal text, usually by two actors. The technique, like theatre games (Spolin, 1986), is the wellspring of creative imagination. Many directors improvise scenes like the ones in a new play before actually reading the play. Improvisations around the plotline, but without the author's words can make the intentions of the characters and the necessary through-line of the play more obvious. For the singer, improvising on the intentions of a song will clarify what it is he is actually trying to express.

Indicating. Overacting through a series of conventional gestures. If the inner life or the reason for the gesture is absent it becomes cliched and hackneyed. For example, a hand over the heart for "I love you."

Intentions or objectives. Every character in a theater piece has something he or she wants. Other characters appear and thwart that intention, which forms the dramatic tension of the piece. The objective or intention of the character forms the subtext, the character's reason for saying and doing the things he or she does. It is usually stated as "I want her love," "I wish to have his respect," and so forth. Subtext is very important in performing songs that are difficult to relate to.

Modes. (Balk, 1991, 214-339). Three modes of acting projection— hearing/vocal, facial/emotional, and kinesthetic—can be individually manipulated in an outside-in method of acting.

Music-theatre. More than theatre with accompanying music. A form that unlike a play, allows time to expand vertically as well as horizontally. A play has one action following another in some type of regularity that leads to a conclusion. Music-theater action often stops (aria) while a character comments on what has gone on before or how he or she feels. It is this narrative stasis that most bores people with short attention spans and that creates the most trouble for music-theater performers. Not only do words and thoughts occur rather slowly in music, so that they must be acted in a sort of slow motion, but the character must hold the stage for a long time by him- or herself.

Presentational. (Kahan, 1985, 13) Theatrical style that recognizes the audience and may play to them. Most of the theater of the past— Shakespeare, Moliere, Greek drama—is in this style. Musical comedy and opera use this style.

Private moment. (Easty, 1981, 107-111) An Actor recreates in public what he or she has only done before in private. It is the final test for complete concentration.

Representational. (Kahan, 1985, 12) A play is a representation of life. An imaginary fourth wall separates the actor from the audience. Most contemporary drama, television, and movies use this style.

Research. Any study that gives depth to an acting project. Dustin Hoffman spent weeks in an institution observing savants before making *Rainman.* Musicians consider most of these items when studying to build an interpretation.

Sense memory. Exercises which force you to remember all the input from the five senses. They generally begin by asking you to describe objects you have seen for only sixty seconds, sounds you just heard, and so on. Further exercises ask the student to feel the warmth of the sun, the pain of a toothache, and so on. If you can adequately re-create the sensations then you can relay them to an audience. When coupled with a vivid emotional memory, they form the most potent techniques of the method.

Style. A term of paramount importance for the singer-actor. Style, as defined for theater, is the behavioral characteristics shared by the play's characters. Those characters determine the style of everything around them as well. For example, in Restoration theater, the most erotic part of a young man's body to a woman was his calf. Therefore, when a rake wooed a maid in a play he often put his foot up on something to show off his calf. Many Restoration paintings show just that posture. It has the same effect as Stanley Kowalski taking off his shirt in *A Streetcar Named Desire.* The intention of the character is the same—to inflame the girl's passion—but the style is different. This is important to the singer, because we play styles all the time when we observe the conventions of recitals, auditions, and serious concerts. Playing a style does not limit the singer's ability to communicate; it only establishes the rules and conventions by which he or she must play. When considered this way, it is easier to understand why we do not dance around the stage like Madonna when we we sing an aria from the eighteenth century. We are conforming to the style of the music, not the performance expectation of an unsophisticated public.

Subtext. Songs are difficult to act because the text is expressed much slower than the rhythm of speech. It is much like trying to stay interested in someone who is speaking very slowly. If slow-paced lyrics do not fire the imagination, then a new text must be devised that will. This new text constructed of the singer's inner thoughts and feelings forms a silent dialogue. "Think of 'sub' in subtext not as meaning below the text, but 'sub' as in substitution. In subtext we substitute thoughts, feelings, emotion, and even dialogue." (Silver, 1985, 23)

Subtexting

Subtexting in a song is an outgrowth of the original Stanislavski acting tenet of objectives. An objective helps the actor clear away the clutter of time and circumstance to concentrate on what he or she hopes to accomplish in a scene. Likewise, a subtext in a song can enrich its performance by adding meaning and direction to what is sung. In Fred Silver's *Auditioning for the Musical Theater* he outlines four useful methods for adding subtext to songs. The following is an application of those principles to different—and I hope useful—examples to the beginning singer.

Subtexting requires the use of an acting partner. The acting partner may be active (that is, he or she may be feeding you dialogue) or passive (just listening attentively). Subtexting and the use of an acting partner are particularly helpful to the singer in filling the air or rests in the song and in giving the song a context for acting that the actor/singer did not have before. This is particularly helpful if the singer has difficulty relating to the text. Many art songs and arias have this problem because they present us with situations that are beyond our experience and understanding.

There are basically four types of subtext: subtext with a passive partner; subtext with an active partner; stage directions; and actor's monologue.

Preparations for Subtexting

Make certain that you can answer all the questions about the song found in the previous chapter. Get a notebook and write out the lyrics leaving two spaces between each line. Add dialogue in the empty lines of your notebook that help you motivate the text or situation. Make sure the dialogue is active with emotions that cause a physical reaction in the singer. Saying "I am sad" usually won't work because the audience only knows that you are sad if you look sad. Inner emotions are impossible to play.

Example of Passive Subtext Insertion
Love Walked In by George Gershwin (lyrics in italics).
I really don't believe in love at first sight, but there I was trying to look interested in the dullest guy at the party when *Love walked right in and drove the shadows away*. I could feel myself staring and starting to smile all at the same time. *Love walked right in and brought my*

sunniest day. It's funny how you can feel so many things for a person you don't even know in just a few seconds. *One magic moment and my heart seemed to know, that love said "Hello."* I thought to myself, "If he speaks to me I'll probably say something really dumb." *Though not one word was spoken*. Thank God he just glanced at me as he passed by. But even that was enough to make me forget where my date had gone. *One look and I forgot the gloom of the past*. How is it that sometimes you can see a guy and imagine what it would be like to live in the suburbs with him? You know, the all-American dream: two-story colonial, station wagon, golden retriever, and 2.4 children who happen to be the most gorgeous ones on the planet. *One look and I had found my future at last. One look and I had found a world completely new, When love walked in with you.*

Example of Active Subtext Insertion

Nel cor più non mi sento by Paisiello (lyrics in italics and translated). It's late at night. You arrive in your dorm room looking like warmed over death. Your roommate, Bill, is startled out of a sound sleep and says: Geez, what happened to you? You look like your dog died and took your momma with him. <You> It happened again. No matter what I do she always finds something wrong with it. *The heart no more sparkles with youth.* <Bill> Hey, turn off that light, will ya? What the heck are you talking about? <You> *Love, love is the cause of my torment, love is the guilty one.* <Bill> Buddy, that kind of torment looks pretty good to me. Sharon is a babe. <You> Yeah, I know. I should count myself lucky. But love can be tough. *You pinch me, you excite me, you sting me, you bite me. What kind of thing are you any way?* <Bill> I'll tell you what kind of thing it is. It's what makes the world go round. It's what makes you want to get up in the morning. <You> Well, it might be like that when it's new, but when she knows she's got you wrapped around her little finger *Have pity! Love is despair!* <Bill> You're nuts! Shut up and go to sleep. And turn out that light!

Example of Stage Directions

The stage direction technique tries to emulate the kind of overwritten stage directions that you read in some scripts in which the playwright leaves very little to the imagination of the performer. It can be applied to any song but is probably most effective with songs that will be given a theatrical performance. Show tunes and arias used for auditions profit from this kind of external direction. However, the technique has another very constructive use. Often a song intended for recital that has a great deal of inner intensity, but little substance for physical motivation, can be brought to life by rehearsing it as a scene. A rich, tastefully confined recital performance of a song can be acquired by exploring the most florid physical interpretation and then scaling it down. The process of reducing the physical attributes of the scene (getting rid of the movement) is best accomplished over a series of rehearsals. The usual result is that as the larger motions are stripped away, a smaller, internalized, but still observable set of emotions takes their place. The following example is the theatrical expansion of one of the well-known Italian art songs.

Lasciatemi morire by Monteverdi (lyrics in italics and translated).

(Enter left, having had the longest fight with _____ you have ever endured. She has drained all the energy from you and left you slump-shouldered, shuffling, weak. You arrive at the piano as if it were the lone safe haven from her in the world. You look up, contemplating what you will do next). *Let me die!* (clutching the piano, as if a melody from it could bring you back to life) *and what can you do to comfort me in this difficult situation* (your heart suddenly seems as if were going to burst and you place your hand across it), *in this great martyrdom?* (There is no hope, your eyes move to the floor and with one last sigh) *Let me die!*

The Monologue as Subtext

The actor/singer constructs a dramatic monologue that embodies the emotional essence or theme of the song and performs it (silently) as he or she sings the song. Audiences generally are amazed at the emotional depth and creativity flowing from a performer who uses this technique without realizing that the actor/singer's involvement is assured because he or she is acting his or her own play. This technique takes lots of time, but is always successful. It is especially good for singing the overexposed warhorses that everyone already knows; for lyrics in archaic or poetic language like art songs and arias; for works written so well there is little room for you to be creative (truly great works of art); for songs you don't like or can't relate to; and for those beautiful pieces of music that are dramatically bland.

A monologue must be carefully crafted to be successful. The steps are:

  1. Carefully analyze the song in all its emotional parameters, paying strict attention to the questions you

answered in the interpretive phase of preparation.

2. Write the monologue to the song in the same way that you would apply subtext.
3. Sing the song, remembering to act the monologue and its indications rather than the song.

Here is the beginning of a monologue that will be applied to *The Impossible Dream*. Normally the monologue and song are separate in the first phases of construction and combined only in performance. The performance version is shown below. Stage directions are in parentheses, internal monologue in regular type, and song lyrics in italics.

(Sarah and James are walking back from a student senate meeting. It is clear by the energy of his step that James has something to say. Song intro rhythm is matching his stride.) You think I'm afraid to run against that jerk because of what happened to me in high school aren't you? *To dream the impossible dream.* Well, things are different now, you know? (His eyes turn up, envisioning triumph.) *To fight the unbeatable foe.* That jerk thinks he can roll right over anybody and make them suffer for even trying to unseat him. *To bear with unbearable sorrow.* (Posture becomes more erect as he thinks of the strength it will require.) *To run where the brave dare not go.* I know how to stop him. People will not vote for him when they find out what he did. *To right the unrightable wrong.* (and so on)

The silent dialogue of a subtext is capable of unlocking the singer's imagination, and imagination is the soul of the actor's art.

Portions of this section on Subtexting are from Richard Davis, "Once More, With Feeling" *Choral Journal* 37 (March 1997): 37-40. © 1997 by the American Choral Directors Association, P.O. Box 6310, Lawton, Oklahoma 73506-0310. U.S.A. Used by permission.

The Third Line

The third line is a term that has been used among opera professionals for some time. It refers to the unwritten interpretive line constructed by the singer to accompany the text and music of an opera. It's the performer's guide to the expression of the work. Because it has never been developed in print, the term has always been amorphous. It's one of those things performers do but have difficulty articulating to someone else. A wonderful book by Daniel Helfgot (with William O. Beeman) has changed all that. In *The Third Line: The Opera Performer as Inter-*

preter, the authors define the third line, codify its parts, and present examples using their system.

> The third line is, briefly, the interpretive line a singer adds to the other two lines in an operatic score. The first line is the text of the libretto. The second is the musical line. The third line is one the *singer* adds and consists of the body movement, eye focus, facial expression, and inflection that make the score leap off the page and into reality on the stage. The third line is the singers' considered conclusion as performers—their visual, physical, mental, and vocal answer to the tasks set for them by the composer and librettist. (Helfgot 1996, 6)

Although singing an aria is not within the realm of the beginning singer, the method used for study illuminates a way of thinking about singing that could be used on any song. For that reason I will give an overview of the method and present as an example a short excerpt from the recitative to Mozart's *Deh vieni non tardar.*

The criteria for study include the notation of musical events in the score that have dramatic or interpretive impact, textual elements, dramatic intent, and the expressive interpretation of the foregoing elements. The purpose of the exercise is to seek meaning in even the smallest elements of the score and arrive at a written system of symbols that when applied to the music will aid the singer's memory. As always, preparatory work includes thorough study of the music, text, and historical context of the piece. For the example used here several sources were found in the library (Moberly, 1968, 132-135; Levarie, 1952, 209-218; Allanbrook, 1983, 174-177; Mann, 1977, 430-433). In addition to the library study, a full score should be used and a word-for-word translation added to the score. The piano vocal score (Figure 3.1) is used here to save space.

Great art works all have one thing in common. The combination of techniques used to produce them can yield many different meanings depending on which layer of technique strikes you as most interesting or how those layers of technique interact. In looking at a great painting you may notice (or *attend to,* as the psychologists say) the delicate detail of the brushwork, the use of chiaroscuro, the elegant use of foreshortening, an interaction of the characters in the picture that tells a story, or just that it's in an interesting picture frame. In music one hears the interaction of the melody with harmony, the use of timbres to create moods, melodic variation to change a musical idea, or just that it has a good beat. Whatever you notice defines the meaning you take away from the work. People who notice only that the picture is in a pretty frame or that the music has a good beat are insensitive to the other techniques displayed in the work. The meaning they take away is fairly simple. The artistically sensitive will not only notice the other techniques displayed but will be intrigued by how they interact to produce a complex meaning. For the third line analysis we will attempt to derive meaning by summing the layers of technique into a meaning-filled expressive outcome. The following analysis begins by defining and describing the area of study: what the singer sees. The numbers refer to the numbered areas on the score. The next area of analysis is what the singer thinks. It examines the layers of the score in this order: music, text, drama, and expression. The third area of analysis is what the singer writes in the score to remember the outcome of the whole analysis.

The singer sees:
1. A lyric melody in first violin is accompanied by a rocking ostinato in second violin and a chord tone from viola. Tempo marking is allegro vivace assai.
2. Cadence of the prelude on C.

The singer thinks:
Music Analysis. This is a 2+2 antecedent-consequent phrase in C major. Very classical. In itself it is not so unusual, except that it is the recitative for Susanna, a servant. The hierarchy observed in most operas of the Classical period, and in most of Mozart, was to reserve accompagnato recitative and complicated melodies on lofty themes for the nobles, while servants received secco recitative and simple melodies on mundane or frivolous subjects. Figaro, also a servant, has an accompagnato recitative *(Tutto è disposto)* just moments before this one. Is it possible the composer is making a musical statement about the ennobling of our characters?

Another clue about the nature of the recitative may be found in the history of the aria. The aria was written for Nancy Storace, a pretty singer whom Mozart was very fond of. In the 1789 Vienna revival, the role of Susanna was taken by Adriana Ferraresi, and a new aria was added for her in place of *Deh vieni*. Many writers feel that *Al desio* lacks the passion of *Deh vieni*, perhaps because Mozart did not feel the same way about the singer. Perhaps Mozart liked Ferraresi and wrote a more interesting recitative for her.

Textual Analysis. No text.

Dramatic Analysis. In the garden of the palace; a chilly and, at least at this moment, very dark night. In the prior scene with Marcellina and the Countess I have discovered that Figaro is here waiting to ambush me with the Count. He doesn't know that I am just the bait to trap a rat (*droit du seigneur* be gone!). I decide to tease my new husband into a jealous rage by singing what he will think is a sensuous aria to the advancing Count. In most productions I am wearing the Countess's dress. In this production, because it's dark and the audience might not assume that Figaro could identify me by voice alone, I will ask the director to leave me in my wedding dress and veil. That way there can be no doubt in Figaro's mind (or a sleepy audience's) that I am Susanna and that he is about to become a cuckold. I will do a quick change after the aria into the Countess's dress. The idea that I could put something so big over on Figaro on our first night together excites me almost to giddiness. These men really are so dumb, and so dear!

Expressive Analysis. The ticking figure of the second violin tells me that motion is implied. I will cast a glance toward Figaro, and make my way downstage by the fountain. My face reflects the delighted impishness of a child, and I can barely keep from laughing. Was sixteen this much fun? Because it is an active introduction I will keep the energy going by entering right on the beat at 2.

The singer writes:

at 1. Spot Figaro and walk downstage to fountain. Face bright. Focus between audience and Figaro.

at 2. A down arrow (indicates that I enter on the beat).

The singer sees:

3. Angular recitative.

The singer thinks:

Music Analysis. The music leading to my first line is precise and energetic. I will keep that energy going by staying close to the beat. Because I think this first line is declamatory and meant to be heard by Figaro, I will not soften the cadence with an *appoggiatura*. The appoggiatura would be indicated by the courtliness of the accompanied recitative, but a blunt ending is more commanding. I will sing mezzo forte.

Textual Analysis. I'm telling Figaro that this is the moment he has been waiting for. I'm beginning the tease by letting him think he was right. I will stress the *g* in *Guinse* to give it more strength. If I observe the Colorni rules the final *o*'s will be open.

Dramatic Analysis. As above. Motivation: I want to make this rich enough to choke him.

Expressive Analysis. Less is more. I could raise my clutched hands to below my chin or do a little turn to express my giddiness, but I think I'll just try to let the my voice and face do the work

The singer writes:
at 3. Bright and measured.

The singer sees:
4. Eighth rest.

The singer thinks:
Music Analysis. A short rest in the middle of a text phrase of recitative should not be thought of as a real stop. The thought of the line, "the gesture" must continue, even though no sound is made. This rest and the one at number 8 serve a couple of purposes. The first is to put a little daylight after *momento* and *affano* to give them some stress. The second is to point up the three sound rhymes of the *o*'s in *momento, affano,* and *mio.*

Textual Analysis. None.

Dramatic Analysis. Sustain the the feeling and the forward motion of the line through the rest.

Expressive Analysis. Any movement or change of focus here will break the line apart, so I will appear as if I am singing through the rest.

The singer writes:
at 4. A horizontal arrow pointing right (join the phrases).

The singer sees:
5. Recitative.

The singer thinks:
Musical Analysis: This is a simple rising third propelled by two sixteenths. There is no accompaniment, so I could take more time on *drò* and warm the tone up so it will really sound like I'm ready to enjoy myself. A little decrescendo on *drò* falling into the next phrase would help put the idea across too.

Textual Analysis. This one of those places where a rolled *r* will help me place the top note and carry energy to it.

Dramatic Analysis. The tease has begun with a vengeance. There is no telling how Figaro may interpret this line, but I want to say it in a way that will send his imagination running wild.

Expressive Analysis. A little tilt of the head, a rise of the shoulders, and downward focus will give the illusion that I am feeling my lover's embrace. I want to portray sensuality by receiving sensation.

The singer writes:
at 5. Tenuto over *drò*. Feel the lover.

The singer sees:
6.and 7. Recitative continues.

The singer thinks:
Musical Analysis. The phrase finishes with a descending line and an appoggiatura. The appoggiatura should be phrased with stress on the non-harmonic tone and de-stress, both of text and dynamics, on the harmonic tone. This gives a little extra feminine lilt to the word "anxiety."

Textual Analysis. *Affano* is receiving its stress melodically. I will give *senza* a little boost by lengthening the first syllable a bit and singing the *e* fairly brightly.

Dramatic Analysis. The idea here is to make Figaro understand that I might be capable of any number of unthinkable things, if freed from the cares of what other people thought.

Expressive Analysis. Numbers 5 through 7 should just drip with teasing sensuality. It must be obvious to the audience that I am teasing, and at the same time not obvious to Figaro. This recitative and aria combination, like so many, represents a duality. It begins as teasing, but as I get caught up in romantic feelings it becomes a sincere apotheosis of Figaro (*incoronar di rose*). I must not anticipate the emotions of the aria.

The singer writes:
at 6. Tenuto over *senza*.
at 7. Add the appoggiatura to *-fanno*.

The singer sees:
8. Eighth rest.

The singer thinks:
Musical Analysis. This rest functions like the last one even though it occurs over the string chord. However, I may need just a little breath here.

Textual Analysis. None.

Dramatic Analysis. The best of all worlds would be to just let this rest connect the lines as the last one did. If I need a breath, though, I can make it part of the meaning of the line. A slightly audible breath on the rest could be interpreted as my lover tightening his arms around me. *Expressive Analysis.* This could be played two ways. If I don't need the breath the rest will just leave *affano* suspended in midair. The rest will be short and connecting. I will continue the low focus until I begin the next line. If I take the breath, it automatically pulls me up and out to the audience.

The singer writes:
at 8. Horizontal arrow pointing right or breath mark and an up arrow.

The singer sees:
9 and 10. The third section of the first line of recitative.

The singer thinks:
Musical Analysis. This telling little phrase, because of the downward leap of a sixth and a final appoggiatura, begs for a gesture. It also closes out a line of thought with the clincher of the tease—*I will be in someone else's arms.* Because it is the last part of the line, and I have not taken much out of tempo, I will relax here to make sure the words are going to hit their mark. I will allow just a bit of portamento on the leap of the sixth to accent its sensuality. Not too much portamento; this is Mozart, after all.

Textual Analysis. The operative word here is *arms.* I will give strong tonic stress to *braccio,* but without letting the rolled *r* take too long. The double *ll* of *all* must be a quick flick to the roof of the mouth so that an extra vowel doesn't get inserted before *idol.* Some appoggiatura stress should occur on *mio* with a feminine and fetching off-glide.

Expressive Analysis. What happens here depends on what happened before. If I take an expressive breath, it pulls my torso up and focus out so that I can wrap my arms around myself as I imagine my lover doing. This will occur on the leap of *braccio.* It reinforces the leap and the word. If I don't take a breath, there isn't enough breath to spend much time on *braccio,* so I will delay the movement of my arms until *mio.* The rising arms will lead to the breath.

The singer writes:
at 9. Tenuto over *brac.* A line joining *all* to *idol.*
at 10. Mark appoggiatura with tenuto.

The singer sees:
11. The same four bars as the introduction.

The singer thinks:

Musical Analysis. This music is the same as the introduction. For me it is a change of beat. I go from the excitement of being in my lover's arms to being shy. I will ask the conductor to play these bars rather more softly and with some hesitation in the violin part. Their rhythm in the final bar would reinforce my changing mood if it were *détaché.* I would also ask for a slight ritard and a tenuto of the last note. I will enter *p* after the cadence.

Textual Analysis. None.

Dramatic Analysis. This change of beat has a full four bars to unfold. I will continue to be excited through the first two bars and transition to shyness over the next two bars.

Expressive Analysis. The first two bars find me in the same posture as number 10. During the second two bars I will let my arms slowly fall, and my face will change from glowing expectation to apprehension with focus straight out.

The singer writes:

at 11. Change of beat from elation to shyness.

This short example will give you an idea of the thought processes that go into an effective interpretation. This need not become a long written exercise for every song you sing, but doing it a few times will get you into the discipline of thinking about all your options. In the end, just as in acting, it is the imagination of the performer that brings the words to life.

Deh vieni, non tardar

Allegro vivace assai   W. A. Mozart

Figure 3.1
Mozart's
Deh vieni non tardar
from *Le Nozze di Figaro*

brac- cio all i - dol mi- o.

Memorization

Memorizing music comes easily to some students and only with great difficulty to others. Memory problems are compounded by sophisticated literature that presents problems with foreign language, technique, and interpretation all at the same time. These problems can be avoided, or at least ameliorated, by developing metacognitive abilities and strategies based on the information-processing model of learning.

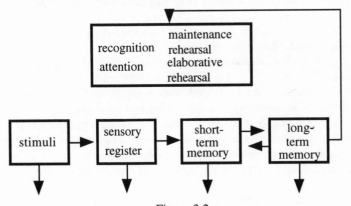

Figure 3.2
How We Process a Memory

The information-processing model of learning has its roots in the flow charts used to diagram computer functions, and is derived from the work of several theorists (Atkinson & Shiffrin, 1968; Gagne, 1985). It defines memory in terms of encoding, storage, and retrieval. In Figure 3.2, environmental stimuli coming to us through our senses (the music we see, the accompaniment we hear) is initially recorded in the sensory register for one to three seconds. In this short period, we either attend to the information (concentrate on its details, trying to perceive a meaningful whole) or recognize it (relate it to something we already know). Information from long-term memory plays a crucial role in determining what will proceed to short-term memory and what will decay and disappear. According to Neiser (1976, 79), "perceivers pick up only what they have schemata for, and willy-nilly ignore the rest." Once in short-term memory, which stores about seven unrelated bits of information for about twenty seconds, information is further encoded by maintenance and elaborative rehearsal before being stored in long-term memory. Maintenance rehearsal is repetition or rote learning. Elaborative rehearsal is relating new information to knowledge already stored in long-term memory. Material can be elaborated by organization (a series of tones can be chunked together to form a melody) or by being made more meaningful. Meaningfulness is added when the learner associates the known with the unknown. A new melody can seem familiar because it begins with the same intervals as one already known. Information in long-term memory is stored in data structures called schemata. Schemata, or stereotypes, define standard relationships and predict sequences of events. A musical schemata would be our expectation of tonic following the dominant chord in tonal music.

Forgetting (decay) can occur at any stage in the encoding and storage process, and in fact it must occur. If we remembered all the information that our senses provided, we would soon be overwhelmed by the minutiae of everyday life. Forgetting can also occur because we subconsciously desire it (repression), because performance anxiety promotes it, and because old and new memories can interfere with each other in the retrieval process. The information-processing model allows us to evaluate and predict the effectiveness of anecdotal methods of music memorization.

Much advice for memorizing music can be found in literature for the pianist. Since the time of Clara Schumann and Franz Liszt, pianists have been required to memorize large volumes of musical material for performance. Most of that advice, beginning with Matthay (1926), Cooke (1948), and others into our own time, is speculative and based on a particular teacher's personal preferences and experiences. These systems of memory, although not scientifically based, have been helpful to many students. Here is a summary of several different strategies. Not all of these tactics will apply to the singer, but they all have a familiar corollary in vocal training.

1. Set up proper conditions for concentrated practice. Eliminate distractions.
2. Look carefully at the first musical phrase. Write in an analysis of melody and harmony using whatever system is most memorable to you. Note character markings and unusual features like truncated part-writing.
3. Close your eyes and visualize the measures with all

your markings. Still with your eyes closed, follow whichever of the next procedures seems beneficial to you. Sing each line through from top to bottom of the score. Write out the score on paper, or etch it in the air. Recite the pitch names in each line or sing them on solfeggio.

4. Play first the right hand then the left in the air with your eyes closed.
5. Play the right hand and then the left at the piano, eyes open, slow speed.
6. Play hands together, slow speed.
7. Check score, repeat at normal speed.
8. Limit repetitions to five. If more seem to be needed, review all the preceding steps first. Rote learning, dependent as it is upon kinesthesia and tactile response, is insufficient for the rigors of performance.
9. Continue to add small sections to your memory repertoire until the whole piece is memorized. Each bit of memory work will require review on a daily basis until the piece as a whole is easily retrievable. Think through the memory piece just before falling asleep each night and upon waking in the morning. Memorization, just like technique and sight-reading, must be practiced every day.

Although the above strategy is not scientifically derived, it does illustrate tactics that are recognizable to memory theoreticians. You will probably recognize these terms from your psychology class. Number one is stimulus attenuation. Number two is elaborative rehearsal, association (adding meaningfulness to something or linking something unknown to something known), and organization. Number three is imagery and transferring visual to aural encoding. Number four is imagery and kinesthesia. Number six is a kind of chunking and flow control (slow speed). Number eight is rote learning and a method for avoiding cue interference. The advice in number nine to memorize before falling asleep at night and review in the morning has been verified by research (Wilson, 1983)

This method will serve for learning the music that you will perform. It will not give you much help for learning the texts, however. For text memory we will rely upon processes as yet undefined by neuropsychologists, and some research data from the field of information processing.

Text can be learned in basically two ways: as repertory memory (Intons-Petersen, 1987) apart from the music, or as a primed response to the music. That is, we can learn the poem in the same way we would to recite it for an audience, or we can use musical cues from the song to retrieve it. The song and text themselves usually determine which method works best. A narrative, perfectly metric poem in a strophic song is most easily memorized using the repertory method. Blank verse that is described by its musical setting will most easily be remembered using the priming method. Here are the steps in the repertory method.

1. Read the poem.
2. Set optimal chunk size (determine how much you can remember at a time and try to hold on to no more).
3. Set retrievability criterion (how well you have to know it and at what depth of comprehension).
4. Rehearse the chunk. If it passes the criterion, continue with the next chunk; if not, re-rehearse.
5. After learning several chunks, loop back to the beginning, and run through all of them.

Repertory memory can be accomplished strictly by rote (just repetition) or by organizing and adding meaningfulness to the text (Noice 1992). Organizing the text might include dividing it into sections based upon the speaker, subjects being described, internal emotional states, grammatical landmarks, or poetic constructions. Meaningfulness can be added by determining the motivations and intentions of the author and by exploring underlying and concomitant meanings. For songs in a foreign language this usually entails first memorizing a translation of the text. The payoff in adding meaning to the text is that it will enrich the overall performance.

For many singers, particularly visual learners, using a system of enhanced imagery is a useful device. Almost any song can be turned into a video in your mind that can be played as you sing.

Mnemonic devices, which are most useful for remembering lists, can be used to cue text learned by the repertory method (Pressley, Levin, & Delaney, 1982). For instance, you could form an acronym (a word composed of the first letters of first lines) from the poem. You could form an acrostic (a sentence made from words derived from first letters of poetic lines). You could use an object mentioned in a line of text as your cue for the line and remember those objects in succession by associating them with objects viewed on a mental walk through your home (loci method). You could link those object cues one to another by constructing a story that includes all the items in succession (story method). You could store the same object cues via the peg-word system. The pegs are: one is bun, two is shoe, three is tree, four is door, five is hive, six is sticks, seven is heaven, eight is gate, nine is line, and ten is hen. If the language of the poem is not your own, choose a single word for each individual line to which you can attach a unique key word (key word system) and rely on rote memory for the rest of the words in the line. For instance, a poetic line in a Schubert song is *"Bächlein, lass dein rauschen ein."* (little brook rush no more) Use the word *Bächlein* (little brook) as your key word. When you come to that line, think of a small portrait of Bach (Bächlein) rushing down a little brook. The ridiculous image will make the line unforgettable.

The method of memory that relies on the priming effect of the music to recall the text is most often used by advanced singers. It naturally lends itself to more communicative and meaningful performance because it is based upon understanding the subtle, nonverbal shades of meaning that music adds to a sung text. It is those nonverbal shades of meaning, applied through musical syntax, which supply the musical cues to retrieve the text? The unfortunate problem with this method is that we observe it every day, but no one could say exactly what features in any particular place in the music remind them of the text. Was it the half cadence, the seven-six suspension two bars ago, the unexpected substitution of a secondary dominant, the overall arch of the melody just prior to the entrance, or the incorrect voice leading in the tenor line that brought the singer in on the right text. Even if we could define what the cues are for ourselves, it would probably not apply to anyone else's musical sensibility.

Having differentiated the two methods of text memory, one should not conclude that they operate exclusively in any one song. Most students use some combination of the two methods depending upon their own cognitive style. For instance, in the repertory method some learners do best by simply thinking through the repetitions, others like to write out repetitions, and still others memorize best by reading the text out loud or rehearsing it with a partner like dialogue in a play. Learning always depends as much on the characteristics of the learner and the material being learned as it does on the activities that lead to the learning.

Retrieval, remembering, is state and context dependent. We remember much better when our internal state is the same during retrieval as it was during encoding (Eich, 1980). In addition, we remember much better when we are in the same physical environment we were in when we memorized (Smith, Glenberg & Bjork, 1978). This is part of the reason that memory fails when students try to perform in an emotional state (high anxiety), or physical space (a hall) that is different from the one they learned in. Your best exam scores come when the room is the same for test and lecture. Your best performance comes when your practice is as close to the performance as you can make it.

Current knowledge on how to memorize, when viewed as gestalt, is really an amalgamation of research results on many topics in many disciplines. For instance, studies have shown that pianists memorize more quickly when instructed in musical analysis (Ross, 1961), and when allowed some time to silently analyze the music before recalling it. Singers memorize more quickly in interactive environments (Williamson, 1964). Pianists seem to profit markedly in memorization when they visualize the score, and those who sight-read easily memorize more easily (Nuki, 1984). Students who are adept at remembering and echoing nonwords are the best at learning foreign languages (Pagano, Valentino, & Baddeley,1991). Experiments on the relationship of text to music have shown that even among nonmusicians there is a very high level of integration between the two, but of course they don't know why (Serafine, Crowder, & Repp, 1984). Memorizing music before bedtime is superior to memorizing after waking (Wilson, 1983). And finally, a new area of inquiry into the relationship of mood to memory and cognition is producing many theoretical constructs that may eventually help the performer (Kuiken, 1991).

Further reading on the subject of theoretical memory can be done in the basic journals of the discipline.

Journal of Memory and Language
Journal of Experimental Psychology: General
Journal of Exp. Psychology: Learning, Memory & Cognition
Journal of Exp. Psychology: Human Perception & Performance
Journal of Memory and Cognition
Cognition and Emotion

College-level psychology and educational psychology texts provide excellent overviews of memory study. The most up-to-date summary of current research is *Perspectives in Memory Research* edited by Michael Gazzaniga and published by MIT Press. A well-known book of the biology of memory is *The Neuropsychology of Memory* edited by Squire and Butters.

A classic how-to book on memory that concentrates on how to remember lists, names, and facts is *The Memory Book* by Lorayne and Lucas.

Portions of this section on Memorization are from Richard Davis, "Memorization for the Young Singer" *NATS Journal* 51:1, 9-11. ©1994 by the National Association of Teachers of Singing, 2800 University Blvd. N., JU Station, Jacksonville, FL 32211. Used by permission.

Performance Anxiety

Picture it. The stands around the baseball diamond are full on a hot hazy afternoon. You march out to center field with your wireless mike, ready to sing *The Star Spangled Banner* to the largest live audience you will ever perform for. The Hammond organ cranks out the intro. You raise the mike to your lips, conscious of 100,000 eyes upon you. You take a deep breath, and . . . and . . . panic! Your mouth is as dry as the Sahara. Your hands are sweating so much you're losing your grip on the mike. Your knees have the consistency of grape jelly. You can't remember the words and begin making up your own. The fans start to laugh, and falling litter begins to collect around your feet. You're a national laughing-stock in three minutes.

While this scenario may sound a little far-fetched, it actually did happen to Robert Goulet. He said afterward that he had always feared "going up" in front of a big crowd, and in fact it is a recurrent nightmare among all varieties of live performers. The very exhilaration that attracts us to live performance can also supply the emotional energy to block our memory, cause us to freeze up, or do things we would not normally do during a performance.

When stage fright—or performance anxiety—as psychologists call it becomes so severe as to curtail performance, professional intervention is usually recommended. Psychologists who treat performance anxiety are of two varieties: psychoanalysts and cognitive/behaviorists. The psychoanalysts generally assume that anxiety is intrapsychic and requires lengthy treatment to uncover the trauma and/or inhibitions that contribute to anxiety. The behaviorists are mostly interested in modifying a stimulus-response pattern that has the potential to do the organism (us) harm. Both types of treatment work, but they achieve the goal of managing anxiety in very different ways.

The cognitive/behaviorists subscribe to a model that says that a trigger (singing a recital, performing heart surgery, arguing before the Supreme Court) yields anxiety (a feeling that coming events are uncontrollable and unendurable). Anxiety can produce either a cognitive response that is composed of a negative inner dialogue (I'm not a good singer, my patient is going to die, and so on) and/or an autonomic nervous system response (muscle tightness, perspiration, palpitations, fight-or-flight syndrome). When both reactions happen at the same time, they have a tendency to feed off each other. The more negative the inner dialogue gets, the worse the physical reaction. The worse the physical reaction gets, the more negative the dialogue gets until a state of complete breakdown occurs (Nagel, Himle, & Papsdorf, 1981).

Behaviorists try to break the stimulus-response pattern, not by removing the stimulus of the anxiety producer (recital), but by altering the subject's reaction to it. Behaviorists and cognitive behaviorists use a wide variety of single therapies and therapies in combination to reduce performance anxiety. Some of the most useful are listed below.

Systematic desensitization. A list of threatening performance images given by the subject is arranged in order from least to most distressing. A progressive muscle relaxation technique is taught whereby muscles are alternately tensed and relaxed beginning with the hands and arms, moving to the head, and finally down to the toes. The subject uses the technique to relax and is then asked to visualize the progressively distressing performance scenes without allowing muscle tension to intrude. Treatment is successful when the most distressing images do not arouse muscle tension (Reubart, 1985). The treatment can be practiced by visualization but is even more effective when the situations are experienced in vivo. This procedure—exposing a phobic individual to the most feared situation or object for an extended length of time without the opportunity for escape—is called flooding (Atkinson et al. 1993).

Implosion. The therapist constructs scenarios of performance based upon what he or she believes will produce extreme anxiety in the student. The student visualizes those scenes in great detail over a protracted period. Eventually those scenes, because of their familiarity, are regarded as absurd. The line between fantasy and reality is redrawn, and the student is less anxious.

Behavior rehearsal and modeling. This is essentially what goes on in studio class. We rehearse the behavior we want during our performance onstage in the friendly, non threatening atmosphere of the studio class, making extinct any negative stimulus/response habits we may have. We model our performance on the best performance characteristics of our peers. This includes the way our peers handle anxiety.

Attentional training. Negative, self-deprecating internal dialogue is changed to positive dialogue. Instead of saying, "If I'm not good everyone will hate me," substitute "I'm going to do my best because it's more fun for me to do so. I am no less of a person if I don't live up to someone else's expectation." The quintessential rule for inner dialogue is that it builds self-worth.

Autogenic therapy. In this therapy, which is allied to self-hypnosis and sometimes referred to as western yoga, the student evokes a state of deep relaxation through the repetition of phrases like "My arm is heavy" and "I feel relaxed." (Ely,1991) Once in this state, the student can change the phrases he or she is repeating to ones that express a positive and reinforcing outlook on performance (positive inner dialogue). The effect is much like hypnotic suggestion.

Cognitive therapy. Essentially any threat is only what we perceive it to be. If we alter the perception of the threat, either by comparing it to some real threat or altering our worldview to accept the threat as no longer formidable, anxiety can be managed. This extremely broad therapy includes temporarily setting aside thoughts about performance, reducing the threat of the performance by changing the meaning of it, and reappraising the reasons for anxiety.

Stress inoculation. Building on the work of Donald Meichenbaum, clinical psychologist Sandra Harris (1986) takes students through the four stages of stress—Preparation, Confrontation, During, and After. In the Preparation period, skills training, practice, time management, physical fitness, relaxation, and replacing negative self-statements with positive, realistic ones are important. Each succeeding stage of therapy has its own useful techniques, applied at the time they are most needed.

Thought stopping. When negative performance thoughts intrude upon consciousness the therapist shouts "stop" and reorients the student's thinking in a more positive way. Eventually the student, after becoming sensitive to his or her own inner dialogue, can subvocally shout "stop," and eliminate negative thinking. Although this sounds amazingly simple, it works well. Here are some positive inner dialogues to replace the negative ones:

1. I will perform for my own pleasure, without letting

the audience determine how I should feel about my performance.

2. The audience is on my side. They want me to sing well.
3. I am ready for this performance. I am well prepared.
4. Sharing what I know about this piece with an audience is a pleasure.
5. I may not give a perfect performance, but I can perform with a perfect spirit.
6. My loved ones (insert names) will still care about me, no matter how this performance goes.
7. The course of human history does not hang on what I will sing in the next hour. In fact, in the big picture it won't even affect *my* history.
8. I will forgive myself for making mistakes and won't dwell on them during the performance.
9. My performance is the best gift I could give anyone, because it is a gift of myself.

Humanistic therapies. Client-centered therapies such as transactional analysis emphasize the individual's natural tendency toward growth and self-actualization. Through the group experience, these therapies are especially adept at getting to the real motivations for performing, and clear the cognitive roadblocks to self-efficacy (a good performance).

Physiological strategies. Physiological strategies including biofeedback, relaxation training, and aerobic exercise are useful in the treatment of performance anxiety because a sense of wellness and relaxation are antithetical to the fight-or-flight response. If a state of relaxation, with its attendant low blood pressure, slow heart rate, and relaxed musculature can be invoked prior to performance, then at least the outward appearance of stage fright (sweaty palms, shaky knees, quivering hands) can be avoided. Because the mind and body are highly integrated, a quiet body may also lead to a quiet, well-focused mind. Biofeedback training allows the student to monitor bodily tensions by viewing graphs, hearing tones, or seeing flashing lights. The most common modalities for biofeedback are electromyograph (EMG), skin temperature (TMP), and electrodermagraph (EDG). The EMG sensors are usually placed on the forehead where they register muscle tension via electrical output of the underlying muscles. Galvanic skin resistance, or EDG, as it is now called, measures the change of electrical resistance on the skin (amount of sweat). Skin temperature (TMP) is an objective measure of how much blood flow is getting to the skin. Patients connected to the monitoring devices actively participate in reducing the physical reactions to stress by practicing imagery or progressive relaxation techniques. The instruments advise them of their success. Individuals who regularly engage in aerobic exercise show significantly lower heart rates and blood pressures when exposed to stress than those who do not. Other methods of relaxation via altered states are also included in physiological therapies. Like the therapies above, they require some instruction to be most useful. In fairly common use today are the techniques of Alexander, Feldenkrais, Dalcroze, and yoga, along with generic practice of deep meditation. Some therapists, particularly those trained in physical observation, effectively predict areas of stress just by looking at the patient. Simple, nonmachine biofeedback loops composed of the patient and therapist can work fairly well.

Psychoanalysis. Psychoanalysis the oldest (beginning with Freud), longest, and most expensive of therapies. It assumes that a person's current problems cannot be successfully resolved without a thorough understanding of their unconscious basis in the early relationships with siblings and parental figures. Through techniques such as free association, dream analysis, transference, and interpretation the therapist hopes to lead the patient to full understanding of himself or herself. The strength of this method is that it can uncover subconscious objections (inhibitions) that keep a performer unmotivated to perform or practice. The method treats the whole person. Because the treatment pattern is tailored to the individual, is of long duration, and is time intensive for the therapist, it should be considered only when all other therapies have failed.

Pharmacological therapies. The last professionally sanctioned treatment for performance anxiety is pharmacological. This includes barbiturates, mood alterers, and vasodilators (calcium and beta blockers). This type of intervention, along with self-administered alcohol, is becoming more common among performers even though the health community discourages drug use without symptoms of disease. Recent studies have shown that the use of blockade medications by the vast majority of performers adversely affects performance instead of enhancing it (Gates, 1988). Obviously, in cases where the performer's health is threatened by the act of performance (hypertension or severe neuroses), medication is indicated.

Thus far we have considered interventions that are to be found in the psychological literature. Other types of anecdotal intervention might work just as well, if they are appropriate for the student.

Rituals, superstitions, fate, and religion. These approaches to relieving performance anxiety transfer responsibility for the quality of the performance from the performer to someone or something else. Many singers have a particular ritual they go through before a performance. It may be a relatively simple routine of dressing a certain way, arriving at the theater at a certain time, warming up in a certain place, or having a few minutes of meditation before going on. Some performers have to have their sense of security reinforced by observing certain superstitions in the hall. Actors never say "Macbeth"or whistle in the theatre. Pavarotti finds a bent nail backstage before he goes on. Some performers believe that fate or higher powers are in control of the performance and are relaxed in the knowledge that something else is in control. True believers of most religions are calmed by prayer before a performance.

Imagineering. One of the most powerful forces a performer has is an imagination. Carefully honing a detailed "mental movie" of what your performance will be like and then trying to recreate that movie in the performance can reduce anxiety. It can give you the impression that there really is little to fear once you step on the stage, because you've done it before in your mind. Some performers are calmed by "out of body experiences." That is, rather than looking at the audience as they perform, they imagine themselves to be in the audience enjoying the performance taking place on stage. It's much easier to be calm from a cozy seat in the balcony. Some performers imagine themselves to be a performer they admire. In emulating the idol's professional level of performance they emulate his or her confidence as well.

Satisfying objections. Salespeople spend lots of their training time learning how to sell over the buyer's objections. They learn how to satisfy any doubts the buyer might have by rehearsing effective answers to the buyer's objections before they try to sell the product. So, too, can the performer sell him/herself on the performance by overcoming any conscious or unconscious objections to it. Objections—reasons for not wanting to perform—always function to protect the performer from a perceived threat (Caldwell,1990). It may be an obvious objection like not wanting to perform because of fear of failure or fear of public embarrassment after failure. It may be a less obvious threat like fearing the loss of affection of someone who has always made your success an unspoken condition of continued affection. In any case, analyzing what the particular objections are and answering them in a concrete way will relieve anxiety. This technique, allied with a truthful, sincere evaluation of why the student wants to perform in the first place, is unparalleled as a motivator for learning and practice.

Reality check. Many performers can't work because they set performance goals for themselves that are far beyond their own capabilities—and often beyond anyone's capability. Performers must resign themselves to the fact they can play at only about seventy to eighty percent of their ability during a public performance (Reyman, 1983). Lowering the expectation for the performance will probably allow the student to perform better because he or she will be less tense. Lowering expectations also reduces the amount of self-criticism many performers are prone to after making an error. In performance, self-criticism can be debilitating. The more the student thinks about the error, the more his/her concentration is diverted from the live performance, making more errors possible. Students need to be reminded that self-criticism is a tool for improving practice, not performance. Many musicians, in an effort to "hype" themselves for a performance, make it more important than it really is. Live performance is an ephemeral creature that does not live perpetually in the memory of the audience. Most people will forget the exact details of a performance in minutes and remember nothing of consequence about it in a few days. The course of human history, despite the vain hopes of a musician, will not be changed by a single musical performance.

Reflexivity. A musical performance is an extremely complex set of mental and physical interactions that seem to occur, at least in gifted performances, as effortless and automatic. Performing by reflex is possible only if the material is prepared to the point of overlearning. Overlearning, as represented by harmonic analysis of a composition and improvisation on that harmonic outline, has been suggested as a strategy for reducing performance anxiety among pianists (McCune, 1982).

No therapy as therapy? Performance anxiety is natural. A little is good for a performer and actually enhances performance. Too much training in coping therapies can diminish performance quality (Hamann, 1985).

Stage fright or performance anxiety is experienced by all performers at some time during their career. Performers with mild to moderate cases of performance anxiety will often profit from common-sense, anecdotal cures supplied by the teacher and practiced by the student. When performance anxiety becomes so intense as to seriously diminish performance quality or cause the student to put up roadblocks to performing, then professional intervention is needed. Psychoanalysts, clinical psychologists, and other health care experts offer therapies ranging from classical analysis to biofeedback. The therapy chosen should reflect the depth of the problem, the resources of the performer, and the performer's cognitive style. Multi-disciplinary research on performers' problems with anxiety began in the late 1960s and continues to expand at a rapid rate (Lehrer,1987). Conferences on performance anxiety and publications like the *Journal of the International Society for the Study of Tension in Performance* and *Medical Problems of Performing Artists* have helped disseminate useful theoretical data to therapists who can apply it. This is good news for sufferers of performance anxiety. A day may come when all performers routinely practice easy-to-learn techniques which keep them free of the symptoms and effects of performance anxiety.

Portions of this section on Performance Anxiety are from Richard Davis, "Performance Anxiety" *American Music Teacher* 44:1, 24-27. ©1994 by the Music Teacher's National Association The Carew Tower, 441 Vine St. Suite 505, Cincinnati, OH 45202-2814.

Auditions

"Competition is for racehorses."

—Bartok

Nothing elicits more fear and dread from a performer than an audition. The thought of having to prove to an authority by a display of talent and skill that we are worthy of a job, an honor, a prize, a role, a seat in the class, or a spot in the choir is onerous. Why is it that every apple on the tree has to be compared before someone makes a pie?

The answer is simple, but not very comforting: there are lots of apples and very few pies. Auditions are a fact of life for performers at all levels. The most renowned professionals and the rankest beginners all have to prove to someone that they are artists worthy of the world's attention.

Since auditioning is a fact of life, let's examine some of the attitudes that make it difficult to audition, and reshape them to improve our chances of succeeding.

1. Auditions are difficult because we are taught from early childhood that we have an inherent, inviolate self-worth. There is no need for competition because eve-

ryone is worthy and equal. Having to ruthlessly compare ourselves to others damages that concept of self-
worth. Rejection is taken personally, because it is
construed to mean that we are not as good as we
should be and that everyone is not equal. Our *reshaped
response* should be that auditions are about the business of finding the right person for the task. They are
incapable of evaluating the worth of the whole person. Rejection merely means that at the moment of
the audition the performer was not what was sought.
It is impersonal. It is comforting, and absolutely essential to the continuation of our culture, that we regard everyone as worthy and equal. This does not
mean that everyone is worthy and equal in *every* facet
of their character, personality, and talent. Whether we
like it or not, we compete for affection, friends, status, and money every day.

2. Auditions are difficult because they seem to fly in the
   face of our ideals about art. The syllogism goes like
   this: We are artists. Art is beyond quantification or
   qualification. Therefore, we cannot be judged. Our *reshaped response* should be that the concept of art as
   an ideal and individual expression of the human heart
   and mind is positively beyond measurement. However, the technique and mechanism by which art is produced is definable. One's success at the technique of
   singing or mastery of the material is certainly evident
   at an audition.

3. Auditions are difficult because it seems that there is
   nothing fair or objective about them. Decisions of the
   auditors seem to be made by whim. Our *reshaped response* should be that there is no such thing as a fair
   audition from the viewpoint of the person auditioning. In order to be fair, all the parties involved, judges
   and auditioners, would have to agree in minute detail
   on exactly what skills had to be displayed at the audition. This will never happen. It is more empowering
   to admit that auditions are about submitting yourself
   to bias than it is to rage against inequities.

4. Auditions are difficult because they subject us to an

environment that is not under our control. The auditor
may ask us to sing something we don't know very
well, or sight-read, or change the style of our singing.
We may work with an accompanist new to us. We
may sing in rooms unconducive to a good performance. Our *reshaped response* acknowledges the cardinal rule of auditioning—show yourself at your best.
The best is attained through disciplined work toward
the audition, and controlling as many of the variables
at the audition as possible. For instance, if asked to
do a cold line reading, ask for some time to read over
the part. If the auditor asks you to shape a musical
phrase in a different way, ask for an elaboration of the
instruction.

5. Auditions are difficult because we jump to the auditors' frame of reference. We try to guess what quali-
ties they are looking for and add them to our performance. The *reshaped response* admits that second-
guessing an auditor is impossible. It is always important to get as much information about the audition
as possible and tailor the audition to that information.
If the producers are used to seeing *Carmen* auditions
with the auditioners dressed up like Carmen, then
dress up like Carmen. If you know that movement
auditions will be held the day of the audition, pack
your movement clothes. Waste no energy on suppo-
sitions or rumors you may hear about an audition.
The time and energy anxiety wastes would better be
applied to practice.

Actor/singers are very versatile. They may be called for a wide variety of auditions, each with its own requirements. Below are some of
the audition types, their most likely requirements, and some tips for
succeeding.

Straight Play

A straight play is a theatrical production with only spoken dialogue. The audition requirements are the mechanisms the producers and
directors feel will best uncover the talents and skills needed in the play.
The physical, emotional, and technical requirements will be different for

every character in the play. Audition requirements may be almost anything, but here are a few of the standard ones:

1. Prepared line reading of scenes from the play.
2. "Cold" (unprepared) line reading of scenes
3. Prepared monologues in different styles
4. Interview by the directors
5. Improvisation

In Michael Shurtleff's clever book on auditioning (Shurtleff, 1978) he outlines a strategy for making an audition come alive and catch the notice of directors. This strategy is applicable to all types of auditions, not just for straight plays. His guiding principles for auditions are that you must be noticed before you can show your talent; that the auditors are looking for the range of your talent; that range can often be shown by recasting the audition material; and that auditions require you to make the most dramatic acting choices possible. Here are Shurtleff's "Twelve Guideposts" and some elaboration of them. Some of the tenets found here will help you gain insights into the dramatic possibilities of songs and arias.

Guidepost 1. Relationship. All acting is about illuminating your relationship to someone or something. That relationship is expressed not just by the fact that it exists, but by your emotional feeling toward the person or thing at the time. It is not enough to say "I am his brother" or "I am in love with her," because it does not show the emotional feeling you have at the moment. You can love someone and still have negative feelings about him or her. In fact, acting is just like real life. No emotion is absolutely pure. Emotional changes within and among people are what make them interesting to us. The emotional changes are the result of establishing relationship.

The musical corollary of this idea of changing emotional states can be seen in art songs and arias. The changes from major to minor mode in the art songs of Schubert and the cavatina/cabaletta combination in nineteenth-century opera reflect how quickly emotional states can change in a relationship. The musical changes are an effort to write in the underlying emotional changes.

Guidepost 2. What are you fighting for? All of life is conflict. We always want something, and someone or something keeps us from getting it. This is the basis of dramatic tension. Older acting methods call this finding the goal or motivation for the character's action. It is important that the motivation be active and compelling enough to keep the auditors interested in us. A character in a scene may say he is bored, but boredom must be played without being boring. We must find what the character wants instead of boredom and play that motivation instead. If we work on the idea that everyone wants relationships to yield their fondest dreams, then every acting choice we make is toward making those dreams come true for the character. Those choices are always active and are the key to passion.

In the second act of Verdi's *Rigoletto*, Rigoletto is constantly warning the maid and Gilda about keeping the door locked and never admitting strangers into the house. His ostensible motivation is to keep his beautiful daughter safe and secure while he is gone. What he is really fighting for is much more passionate. Gilda is the living memory of his dead wife and the only pure and unspoiled thing in his life. By keeping her safe and pure he redeems his own soul from the decadent life of the ducal court he serves. Redemption is the most powerful of motivators.

Guidepost 3. The moment before. Every scene or song begins in the middle. It is up to the actor to give context to the current action by supplying a personal history for the character. All too often scenes and songs fall flat in their first half because the actor has not created an emotional environment for the audience right from the beginning. Knowing who you are and what you are makes a better first impression than forcing the audience to discover you as the scene unfolds. Because musical theater, opera, recitals, and especially auditions present characters without lengthy development, this is particularly important.

An actor can telegraph to an audience what he was doing in the moment before his entrance by using the entrance itself. Kramer in the popular television show *Seinfeld* gives us an idea of what has been happening to him by the way he enters Jerry's apartment on every episode. Every entrance is physically unique and portrays the happenings of the moment before. It's also funny.

Guidepost 4. Humor. Humor and jokes are not exactly the same thing. Jokes are intended to entertain. Jokes abound in the work of Neil Simon. Humor, which may not make us laugh, is the attitude that makes living possible in an unfriendly world. It is the coping strategy of seeing the lighter side of a situation. Like comedy timing, it really cannot be taught. Humor can be found in every scene you play, and in the work of all serious actors. Good examples of humor and comedy from serious actors can be found in cinema between Katharine Hepburn and Spencer Tracy. The admonition to actors playing comedy that "you must not think you are funny" has its roots in the idea that everyone does things that are funny, and the real joke is that we don't know we are doing it.

Guidepost 5. Opposites. "Whatever you decide is your motivation in the scene, the opposite of that is also true and should be in it" (Shurtleff, 1978, 77). Life is an ebb and flow of changing mood and attitudes. In the space of a few minutes we may desperately need someone's approval and then be repulsed by our own need. Parents adore their children one moment and want to smack them the next. It is our inconsistency that builds the dramatic conflicts needed to make us interesting to other human beings. Playwrights may not always illuminate the opposites in a scene with dialogue because they assume the actor will see them.

The concept of opposites is found in theatre theory and in opera theatre theory. In *The Complete Singer-Actor* (Balk 1985,95) the author talks about using opposite attitudes to bring an aria alive, and those attitudes are listed in his later work (Balk, 1991, 391). In "Ah! Per sempre io ti perdei" from Bellini's *I Puritani,* Riccardo is lamenting the fact that Elvira is marrying someone else. The overall mood of the piece is sorrow, but the opposite emotion can be played when he remembers the joys they once shared.

Guidepost 6. Discoveries. Discovery is allied with the Stanislavski concept of "the first time." In every scene and in every performance new things must be discovered to keep the material fresh. The newness can come from new understandings about your character or another's, doing something differently, or even seeing or hearing something new onstage. Canned auditions, just like canned performances, don't sell.

Guidepost 7. Communication and Competition. How often have you heard a friend say "you never told me that" when you are quite sure you did tell him or her? This is a failure to communicate, an example of speaking at someone instead of to someone. Communication is a circle. A message is sent, and if it is received, it is acknowledged in some way and returned to the sender to complete the circle. When the message is sent but not acknowledged by the receiver, all kinds of misunderstandings and their emotional consequences can occur. It is as important to listen to another's lines and respond to them as it is to utter your own dialogue.

No one wants to believe this, but all dramatic relationships, just like our relationships in real life, are competitive. We have healthy competition for money, fame, friends, lovers, and everything else. The audition should reflect the same commitment to competition that is found in real life. Just as it is no fun to play a game with someone who won't play seriously, so it is no good to play a role without commitment.

Guidepost 8. Importance. In the name of living on the stage or in an effort to make their acting truthful, actors very often flatten the drama of a scene. We are so conditioned to avoid conflict in our everyday lives that we think *truth* in drama is represented by mirroring the commonplace. Drama is not about the truth of the everyday and the humdrum. It is about presenting a heightened reality filled with emotion. The audience desires the novelty of someone else's emotional rendition of the truth. What is important to them is seeing what is important to someone else.

Importance is built into a scene by choosing motivations that expose the widest possible emotional palette and illuminate the dreams and aspirations of the character. There is nothing so engaging or intimate as discovering someone else's dreams. In the opening scene of Rogers and Hammerstein's *Oklahoma!*, Laurie works very hard to make it seem as though Curly is not the least bit important to her. But, instead of just going inside and avoiding him, she continues to talk to him. She tells him her dream about going to the dance in a coach pulled by white horses.

Guidepost 9. Find the events. Plays are about *what* happens and *who* happens. The screenplay for *The Terminator* is largely about what happens. The events are physical assaults, homicides, car chases, and fantastic special effects. *The Gin Game* by D. L. Coburn is largely about who happens. Two pensioners in a welfare home court the knowledge of each other's life-shattering failures as they play successive hands of gin.

Events are points of change in a play. They can be a physical action, psychological discovery, or learning a fact that changes the way everyone relates to one another. Events are punctuated by a change in the actor's emotional state—a change of *beat,* as the method actors call it. Without events the play has no forward motion and nothing to keep an audience or an auditor interested.

Guidepost 10. Place. In an audition played on a bare stage, the actor can create the scene anywhere he or she wants since it is purely imaginary. For is a conventional scene it is usually better to choose an environment the actor already knows. The actor should play it in his living room so that it feels comfortable. It is the emotional quality of the environment that lends credibility to the actor's work, not the specifics of the environment itself. Sally Bowles in *Cabaret* can't leave the decadence of 1930s Berlin even though her lover beckons. Her morality is so much the morality of the place, that she would be comfortable and accepted nowhere else. Place is vitally important to understanding why Sally acts the way she acts.

Guidepost 11. Game playing and role playing. Our lives are filled with games and roles that we play. We are sons and daughters to our parents, students to our teachers, and taxpayers to our government. In the role of sons and daughters we play the game of doing everything right so that Mom and Dad will love us. In the role of students we might play at acting out so that the teacher will notice us. The game we play in each role, and the fierceness with which we play it, determines how much we care about the game. What matters to the auditors at an audition is not just that we recognize the role we are playing in a scene, but that we play the game implied by it with intensity.

In the birthday party scene of Sondheim's *Company* we meet all of Bobby's friends. The most powerful and commanding of them is rich and spoiled Joanne. Her game is to insult and demean all the other guests to prove that she is the only friend worthy of Bobby's time. Auditions are improved by playing whatever game is afoot with absolute conviction and commitment.

Guidepost 12. Mystery and secret. All the great stars of the past had something mysterious about them that kept the audience interested in them. It was a quality beyond physical charisma, beyond just wondering what was behind Bette Davis's blue eyes. It was the mystery of never knowing exactly how the actor's character would react to a situation or what kind of relationship she would build with another character. Unpredictability can be added to any scene by choosing an illogical motivation or adding a change of beat that is not really there.

Mystery can be added by playing "I've got a secret." We all have secrets we are desperate to keep and just as desperate to share. Curiosity about ourselves and our peers keeps us forever probing each other. In our probing we hope to discover the inner life of another person, and by our reflection in him or her, discover ourselves.

Act III of Puccini's *La Boheme* is full of secrets. Rodolfo tells Marcello he left Mimi because he was bored. Marcello knows this is not the truth and forces two secrets from his friend: that he was jealous when Mimi was around other men, and that he is guilty about being

too poor to provide a healthy environment for her. Marcello is interrupted before he can squeeze the last and most important secret from
Rodolfo, that he left Mimi because he did not have the courage to watch
her die from tuberculosis.

Audition Dos and Don'ts

1. Do be on time. Do dress appropriately for the audition. Do have all the materials prepared (résumé,
   monologue, picture). Do be courteous and accept direction from stage managers and directors.
2. Do try to be as natural as possible in the interview.
   Faking anything before a director is risky.
3. Do read lines, cold or prepared, with stress toward the
   action words, color words, and phrases that change the
   beat.
4. Do allow an improvisation to be melodramatic. Let it
   continue until you are told to stop.
5. Do choose a monologue that fits a character and emotion that you can play. It doesn't have to be a monologue from a play either; all kinds of literature will
   work. Dramatic poetry, a scene from fiction, and even
   your own writing can be effective. A one-person
   show can be created with play dialogue. You can establish the other characters place onstage and speak
   their lines as well as your own. You can monologue
   a dialogue by placing short silences where the other
   character speaks. In a monologue with an acting
   partner, put your partner downstage with his or her
   back to the audience. Do check the monologue sources listed in Chapter 7.
6. Do something that will get you noticed when things
   are not going well. Play the opposite of the script.
   Alternately blame your acting partner for how badly
   the reading is going and then love him or her, whether it fits into the script or not.
7. Don't memorize the script for an audition unless you
   are directed to.
8. Don't hold complete eye contact with your acting
   partner during a reading. People don't really talk to

each other that way. Don't hold complete eye contact with your imaginary acting partner during a monologue. Establish the partner's place by talking to it a bit, and go about your business. When people talk to themselves or to God, a high focus downstage works the best.

9. Don't try an accent unless you have practiced it.
10. Don't use the stage directions unless they can help you. Often they are miles away from where the scene should be going, and you can't follow directions to sit in a chair when it isn't there.
11. Don't spend any energy trying to figure out why you didn't get the role. Casting is subjective and that is just the way it is!

Musical Theater

The musical theater audition includes auditions for musical comedy, operetta, opera, variety, and talent shows. The most important skill in the audition is singing, but it may include any of the following:

1. prepared line reading of scenes from the show
2. "cold" (unprepared) line reading of scenes
3. prepared monologues in different styles—usually comedy and serious, classic and contemporary
4. interview by the directors
5. improvisation
6. prepared songs of two styles—up tempo and ballad
7. arias in contrasting styles and languages
8. a song or aria from the work your auditioning for
9. a short movement audition

Because this class of auditions is very broad, real-world auditions are likely to include only some items on this list. Musical comedy usually will include 1, 2, 3, 6 and 9. The monologues and prepared songs will be short: sixteen bars for the songs and as little as a minute per monologue. It is not unusual for audition calls for musicals to begin with a "typing" call. A typing call is basically a beauty contest to see if you look and move in a way the directors can imagine the character in the show looking and moving. It is a method of shortening the audition protocol. Why spend time auditioning if the directors think you are too short, too blond, too young, or too something to get the part? The movement part of the audition is usually elementary and may be taught to a group at a separate call. They rarely make use of difficult combinations unless the role calls for lots of dance. It is likely that the movement required must be of good enough quality to blend in with the work of real dancers.

Opera auditions usually include items 7 and 8. Semi-professional auditions may include the "basic five" repertoire—that is, five arias in contrasting styles from the singer's performance repertoire. Usually only one or two are called for in the audition. This style of auditioning is most often found in cattle calls, or auditions that allow many performers to audition without making specific role considerations. When auditioning for a specific opera, generally the arias or music sung by a specific character in the show makes up the audition material. Directors are looking for singing and acting in the audition that is much the same as they would expect to see in the production. In fact, opera directors have a tendency to use little imagination about the potentials of the person singing for them.

Choral or Ensemble

Choral and ensemble auditions are a semester ritual at most college campuses. They may include any of the following:

1. Singing a song of your choosing
2. Range and timbre vocalizing
3. Sight-singing
4. Preparing one of four voice parts and singing it with a quartet
5. Pitch memory drills
6. Rhythm memory drills
7. Movement auditions

Choral auditions will usually include 1, 2, 3, 4, 5, 6 and 7. Show choirs and jazz groups will include 8 as part of the audition. Items 2, 4, 5, and 6 do not require preparation beyond your own experience. The solo song should be presented using all the techniques you have learned. The song needs to show your voice at its best, and generally ensemble directors reward repertoire choices that reflect serious study. Sight-reading can usually be improved by not panicking and working through a checklist of observations before you sing. Scan the whole sight-reading piece, noting key, mode, accidentals, difficult rhythms, difficult leaps, and repeats of material. Using whatever rhythm system you know, count through the difficult rhythms. Ask for the starting pitch or key and sing through the difficult melodic places using whatever system you know. Ask for a tune-up and try to sing through the piece. Often a director will try to help you when you get stuck. Try to use the help even if you feel unnerved. Movement auditions will not usually be too vigorous; nevertheless, wearing loose clothing and warming up the body before you go will help.

Audition Dos and Don'ts

1. Do read the dos and don'ts for straight play auditions. Do look in Chapter 7 for appropriate musical theater songs and monologues.
2. Do stage your singing audition. "The rule I learned, the Goldovsky rule, was that any movement which encompassed the space under your arms, anything that was necessary to convey the character and show that you understood the character, was usable. (Dornemann 1992, 85) Transitions during the song (move during the important rests) and from your entrance on the stage through the song's introduction should be staged. Do find an acting partner to sing to in the room. The best place for him or her is center, just over the auditors' heads. "The effect of our eyes finding and zeroing in our acting partner is the equivalent of the curtain going up." (Silver 1985, 110) "Always introduce yourself and your accompanist. If you have been announced by a person in charge of the auditions, and if the accompanist is not solely yours but someone playing for the auditions in general, then introduce only your selection. Know the correct pronunciation of the title of your selection, and the meaning of all the words you sing. There is nothing more disturbing than the announcement of an Italian aria with a Southern drawl." (Corn & Haupt-Nolen, 1985, iv) Do observe the standard rules of stage decorum in an opera audition. Walk in with confidence. Speak in a stage voice. Do try to work with the ac-

companist before you go on, even if you just sing
through the tricky places with him or her.
3. Do try to stay away from the warhorses in a musical
comedy audition. With only a minute for each piece,
you really have to make the up-tempo and ballad se-
lections distinctive.
4. Don't telegraph your personal feelings during an audition unless they are the same as the character you are
portraying. A grimace when you go for your high
note will always be interpreted as a lack of technique.
5. Don't try to impress with the size of your voice in an
opera audition. You will likely over sing and be considered a poor interpreter.
6. Don't allow fear to take over your instrument. "Let's
face it: fear is real. Denying that will only cause it to
manifest itself in an unpredictable manner, so accept
the reality. But at the same time, you should realize
that some fears are imposed by you yourself, while
others are caused by the situation. If the factor that
causes a particular fear is controllable, advance planning can allay that fear." (Owens, 1984, 30)

Contest and Prize Singing

Unlike the auditions described earlier, contest and prize singing is
laden with rules about repertoire, rules about how to apply, rules about
different phases of the audition process, and rules about who can audition. The reward for complying with all these rules can be immense in
terms of experience and dollars. Once all the criteria are met, a contest
audition is like a music theatre audition, except that the only activity is
singing.

Toward Artistry

A good performance can be the result of following a composite of
directives appropriate to the singer's talents. Here are some of the directives that are most often heard divided into areas of interest for the student.

Learning Music

1. After the mechanical details have been learned, forget

the details and sing the song as if you had composed it.

2. It is generally best to sing all recitatives in a feeling of duple time. This will give a better flow to the recitatives.
3. In difficult passages aim for the accented notes. This is particularly true in the melismas.
4. You should not breathe just because a sentence or musical phrase is broken up by a rest. Observe the rest, but imagine you're singing through it.
5. Always make good use of the adjectives.
6. The bass line in an accompaniment is most important to the singer. Make sure the accompanist plays the bass line clearly, particularly in Baroque music.
7. Always sing through the consonants. Do this by adding final consonants to the word or syllable following.
8. Don't worry about what you sing but what you say. It is the thought that will sell the song. If you express the thought in your voice and follow through with your face and body, the audience will receive the message.
9. In singing *pp* make sure you don't let the intensity of the sound drop. Sing *piano* but support *ff*.
10. In singing a diminuendo keep the breath and support going as if you were still singing *ff*. This will keep intensity in the sound. Try to retain the vowel in crescendo and diminuendo.
11. Sing tenutos and ritards with authority and be sure they are properly prepared so that the accompanist can follow you.
12. Use rubato as you sing without breaking the fundamental beat. Word flow with appropriate stress is what makes text sound natural and interesting.
13. Breathe past the end of the phrase, otherwise the phrase ending may drop. Avoid the grunt release except for moments of high drama.
14. It is sometimes necessary to take a breath in the middle of a long melisma. In such cases repeat the original vowel after entering with a new breath.

15. Emphatic (syllabic) and emotional (key word) stress must be used with care. Every word is not equally important to meaning.
16. The word stress of some songs does not agree with the metric setting of the music. It is a mark of the singer's art to correct and naturalize word stresses so that the ear of the listener is not disturbed.
17. "Line" must be observed in all singing. The ear does not adjust rapidly to soft sounds sung immediately after very loud ones.
18. Recite the text as though it were a dramatic monologue. If you can say it convincingly you can probably sing it that way.
19. Tone must ride the breath.
20. All sustained tones must have life.< >.
21. Do not make a habit of ending every song with a ritard or force your accompanist to ritard before your every entrance.
22. Repeated phrases must always sound different. Note that composers use phrase length and arch as separate parameters for establishing mood. Not all phrases arch.
23. The conscious mind is the center of practice, the unconscious the center of performance.

For high notes observe the following:

1. Relax the mechanism as much as possible. Yawning, head rolls, changing body posture, hooting, lip trilling, humming, deep rhythmic breathing, and a moment of meditation can help release the tension that keeps high notes from working. Remember, it is the correct positioning and coordination of the mechanism that results in an easy sound, not brute force.
2. High pitch sometimes results in fewer physical sensations than low pitch. When learning to sing high notes, reduce volume levels and think of slim clear tone instead of trying to beef it up.
3. Very often the high note is not so much the problem as the note of approach. Slimming up the penultimate note can ease a higher note. A leap to a high

note can sometimes be filled with a portamento in some singing styles (nineteenth-century opera). Sometimes adding the portamento as a practice tool is helpful, even if you can't use it in performance.

Performance Venues

Every student of singing wishes to follow as many avenues for his or her personal performance as possible. Regrettably, not all avenues are safe or in the best interest of the student's maturing instrument. The average undergraduate student is conditioned to sing continuously for only about forty-five minutes at a sitting. Singing a two-hour rock concert, a club set in a smoky room, or a two hour choral concert is just not practical. Any singing condition that requires more than forty-five minutes of vocalization or in a less-than-auspicious environment is cause for concern for the teacher and the student.

Students often ask about the ramifications of choral work for the solo singing voice. Here are some points you might consider:

1. Choral music generally requires singing in a tessitura that is not natural to your voice. This is mostly caused by the fact that voice parts have to be highly separated in the harmonic structure of a piece to sound good, although voices are not made to work continuously in those ranges. Baritones and altos sing too low for too long, and sopranos and tenors often sing too high for too long.
2. Choral music often encourages singing too loud because you cannot really hear how loud you are singing with a group of people. It also encourages you to often sing more softly than you should. This whispering piano very often causes the folds to redden.
3. Choral singers often modify vowels to blend with their fellow singers so much that it becomes a habit in their solo singing.

Having mentioned these points, I will add that I advocate choral singing for the undergraduate singer. When proper precautions are taken by the choral director, ensemble singing can be one of the most rewarding activities of a student's undergraduate career. The choral venue will allow the student to enjoy the work of the great masters before he or she has the technique to sing them as a soloist.

The choral student should always be aware of hyperfunction (too much vocal exercise). He or she should take whatever steps are necessary to guard against it, even if the sentiment for such protection is not highly regarded in your ensemble.

Likewise, any other activity that tempts you to poor vocal hygiene or hyperfunction is suspect. That includes talking over high background noise, shouting, crying, cheering, making funny noises, and singing in rock groups.

Advice on Performing Day

Performance and audition days can be nerve-racking to the most seasoned performer. The strategies for coping with performance anxiety discussed earlier, combined with thoughtful advance planning can help get the most from your performance. While some of these recommendations may appear to be too obvious even to need mention, many performances have been ruined because the obvious was overlooked.

1. Know where, when, what, why, for whom, and with whom you will be singing. Many a performance has been marred because a singer is not really able to answer the five W's.

2. Practice in the venue recreating not only the conditions you expect during the performance but some additional distracting variables as well. For example, if you're going to an open-call audition for a musical, take a friend to make distracting noises or role-play the uptight director.

3. Dress appropriately for the performance venue. Dress in Sunday clothes for recital hearings, juries, and serious public performances. Observe your school's concert attire requirements at school-sponsored events. Wear comfortable clothes you can move in to music theater auditions.

4. Find a sequence and repertoire of performance-day activities that will lead to your best concentration. Obviously, you must be well-fed, well-groomed, and well-rested. Some singers prefer eating before singing, some do not. You must follow the rules for good vocal hygiene. No matter how unusual a preperfor-

mance activity may seem to others, if it harms no one else and supports a good performance, it is permissible. Some common activities are meditation, prayer, light exercise, chatting with someone you care about, or purposely making the day ordinary by doing nothing special at all.

5. Observe the rules of decorum for the performance venue. If it is a formal recital, acknowledge your pianist, and practice your bows, entrances, exits, and stage gestures. If it is a performance as soloist with a symphony or chorus, practice acknowledging applause, and learn the path to your seat, when you go on and off, and in what order.

6. Practice professional treatment of your colleagues. If it is customary to pay the accompanist after an audition or recital, have the check ready before you get there. If backstage gifts are the norm at your school, observe the tradition.

When auditioning for musical theatre, remember that the rules for dress and protocol are very flexible. You may be asked to perform a monologue, read a scene, sing sixteen bars of an up-tempo tune and a ballad, learn a dance combination, be interviewed by the directors, or just walk across the stage to be "typed." The only adequate preparation is to be prepared for anything. The more information that can be garnered about the audition the more specific and successful your presentation can be.

Résumés for musical theatre are different from vitaes and work résumés, in that the important information beyond your personal statistics relates directly to your theatrical experience. It is important to list the roles you have performed, when, and, if a famous person was involved, with whom. Opera résumés may also include the roles that you know but have not yet performed, and with whom you have studied. Most résumés should have a special line for any special talents you might have like juggling or gymnastics.

Recording

Probably one of the most humbling events in a singer's life is to hear how his or her voice sounds on tape. Even recordings with the finest equipment seem to bear little resemblance to how we sound to ourselves. The voice on tape seems tinny and small. What we thought was excellent diction when we recorded may sound unclear, and even the most natural vibrato can sound suspicious. This paradox between how we think we sound and how we actually sound has psychological and acoustic explanations. We all have a self-image that includes the way we sound when speaking and singing. Teenage boys, particularly, when there is a girl around they want to impress, try to sound more virile by lowering their speaking pitch and bassing up the voice. Girls in the same situation will either try to sound very feminine and speak softly at a high pitch, or try a low, sexy vamp sound. The voice is part of the image we choose to project. Because the personality of the speaking and singing voice is the product of imagination, our moment-by-moment assessment of how we sound is based on what we actually hear and what the mind tells us we should be hearing. The difference between these two aspects of perception can be quite large, especially when you add the powerful effect of teacher and peer suggestion to self-image. If someone as knowledgeable as the teacher says that your singing voice has a fine dark timbre, you tend to hear a fine dark timbre when you sing. If the suggestion is strong enough, you may even hear the fine dark timbre when it doesn't exist on a recording. Sometimes singers who appear to be extremely conceited about their singing talents are just echoing the suggestions they have heard from others and are not capable of evaluating their performances independently.

There are acoustic as well as psychological reasons for the differences we hear between our live performances and recordings. Much of the difference has to do with the way sounds (vibrations) reach the ear. When we sing, the vibration of the vocal folds, and its subsequent resonation in the vocal tract, sets up strong vibrations which travel through the air outside the mouth, and through our own bone structure to the ear. Since bone is denser than air, it carries the upper harmonics of phonation poorly. In fact, high spectrum partials are attenuated at a rate 6 db per octave faster in bone than air. The sound reaching the ear through bone conduction is decidedly bassy. In addition, the amount of sound produced in the vocal tract during phonation is about twenty decibels higher than the ear's threshold of pain; that is, a great deal of stimulation is reaching the ear via bone conduction. The sound exiting the mouth is highly directional. Short, high-frequency partials are less able to bend around the structure of the head to get into the ear. Long sound waves from low frequencies bend around to the ear rather well and are more prominent in the sound the ear actually receives. In summation, the sound the ear receives from both methods of conduction is bass oriented. That is why singers always feel their recorded sound is tinny and shallow.

To further add to this perceptual dilemma, singers work in all sorts of different acoustical environments. Each environment will change the feedback received at the ear based upon the room's acoustic properties. Rooms with lots of hard, flat, reflecting surfaces will increase the number of high partials that reach the ear. Rooms with lots of irregular surfaces, or the presence of many damping materials (carpet for example) will limit the number of high partials reaching the ear. This is why so many professional singers advise novices to sing by what you *feel* instead of what you *hear*.

If a singer's perception of his or her sound is so unreliable, how does one learn to sing? The answer lies in accurate feedback systems and mental translations. One of the best feedback systems is the advice of the teacher. He or she becomes our ears in the audience. Other more mechanical systems, while certainly not endowed with any kind of wisdom, can be helpful. Singing into a flat-surfaced corner or cupping the hand over the ear can help. Setting up an electronic fold-back system may be helpful. A simple system would consist of a pair of mikes placed some distance from the singer, connected to an amplifier that drives sound-isolating headphones worn by the singer. These systems make air conduction more prominent than bone conduction. Critically reviewing recordings made of the voice can be helpful, provided that the recordings are of high quality and made without electronic enhancements. Experience will allow the singer to become a translator of aural and physical sensation. One learns to translate what a certain sound in the ear actually sounds like to a listener. Likewise, one can learn to predict the aural outcome of physical sensations that occur during singing.

Students often need to make recordings of their singing for entrance into colleges and universities, for the preliminary rounds in singing contests, and for distant professional auditions. Because the reasons for making the tape are diverse, different recording techniques are needed to ensure that the student represents him or herself well. The importance of the tape should determine how much a student is willing to spend on making the recording. If a tape is very important, then a professional studio, carefully chosen by its reputation with other singers, should be used. If the tape is less important and the student knows about recording, then the student-made tape will suffice. Because many people are not acquainted with resources that are available in the professional studio or have little experience recording themselves, I have included a glossary of studio terms and some materials and techniques for making your own tape.

Professional recording has changed a lot with the advent of digital technology. In the past, a recording engineer relied on an artist who didn't mind a lot of retakes, a few good pieces of equipment, a good recording hall, and years of practical experience to make a first class recording. The current high-tech studio offers digital rather than analog master tapes made through a mix board of at least twenty-four channels with an almost unlimited palette of enhancements. Here are some of them.

Equalization, or "EQ," is the adjustment of various frequency bands in the tonal spectrum. In its most primitive form it is like the tone controls on your stereo. Highly selective parametric equalizers can shift very narrow bandwidths making timbre changes that are very subtle or very radical. EQ'ing is largely responsible for the timbre difference we notice in a professional singer's recordings.

Panning is an effect not much noticed in a simple recording of voice and piano since both instruments sound as though they are being produced in the center of the stereo pair. However, in more complex recordings panning makes it possible to construct a complete soundstage between the stereo speaker pair with some instruments coming from right, left, or center.

Digital reverberation is used to add spaciousness to the recorded sound by mimicking the reflective properties of the interior of a concert hall. A reverb unit adds hundreds of closely spaced, randomly delayed, progressively attenuated copies of the recorded sound to the original sound.

Compression reduces the dynamic range of a performance by making the quiet sounds louder and the loud sounds quieter. This is necessary for two reasons. First, the wide dynamic range of a close-miked singer can be very difficult to track manually, and second, even digital recorders require signal levels within certain minimums and maximums. If a recording is made for commercial use it must be compressed, otherwise the buyer would spend much of the time rolling the volume up and down on his stereo. This would be particularly annoying on a car stereo where external sound would mask all the low volumes levels.

Sound *gateing* cuts all signal to the record deck when it falls below a certain loudness threshold. A limiter reduces the peak levels of sound going to the recorder by compressing volumes above a certain threshold.

Echo repeats a sound after a short delay (50 milliseconds to 1 second). It differs from reverb in that the repeats are fairly widely spaced creating the aural sense of a cavern. Slapback echo (delay of 50-200 milliseconds) was originally created by delaying loops of analog tape and is reminiscent of the early Elvis recordings.

Chorus repeats a sound after a very short delay that varies slightly in duration. It adds shimmer.

Doubling repeats a sound after an extremely short delay (16 to 40 milliseconds). It makes one singer sound like two, giving a fuller sound.

Harmonizing is a sophisticated digital technique that allows one voice literally to sing in multipart harmony with itself. Older models allowed only a fixed-interval, parallel kind of harmony, which meant that some chords just were not in the key. Newer models actually make diatonic chords as they occur in the key. When combined with doubling, the harmonizer set to a short interval of just a couple of cents can make a solo voice sound very rich.

Flanging is a time-based effect that results in a series of peaks and dips in the frequency response and sweeps them up and down the frequency spectrum. It imparts a hollow, ethereal quality to the sound.

A *de-esser* does just what its name implies. It removes excessive sibilance from the recorded sound of *s*.

An *exciter* adds brilliance to a sound by adding just a slight amount of distortion to the top end. (Note that dither generators added to digital systems make digital recording sound more realistic by adding small amounts of distortion to the whole spectrum.)

Looping is the editing process of repeating musical events. Rap backgrounds are created by repeating just a few measures over and over.

Flying in or *punching in* is like using the cut-and-paste function of a word processor. A small section is copied and inserted in the song.

Comping, or making a composite performance, can be accomplished in several ways. The engineer can record several takes and synch them on a multitrack recorder. While playing back all the tracks at once, the engineer selects which track will be part of the final take by turning that track on and leaving the others off the master track. He can also use computerized editing techniques to mark edit points and then paste samples from other takes into it. Commercial recordings may have hundreds of edit points in them. Edits can be accomplished on sound entities as short as a few hundredths of a second. Sophisticated sampling and computer-assisted editing techniques can literally add high and low notes to the singer's voice and replace wrong notes in the performance (punching in).

Analog-to-digital converters change sound into a bit stream by sampling the incoming waveform about 48,000 times a second. Digital recorders store the resulting binary code (usually sixteen bit) and have D/A converters in them to replay the stored information as the music we hear (analog). The result of the process is virtually noise-free tape.

Professional recordings can be a costly undertaking. Full-featured studios may charge hundreds of dollars per hour for their services. Students can make good recordings for themselves at very little cost if they spend the time necessary to learn basic recording techniques. Outlined below is the basic equipment necessary and some simple recording techniques to help you make your first tape. You will nee the following equipment:

- A good hall with fairly uncolored reverberation
- A good piano
- Two microphones. The best quality you can afford. A minimum standard would be the Shure SM 57/58.
- Two mikes stands, the heavier the better, with shock mounts if possible
- A good-quality tape recorder with mike inputs. Many older reel-to-reel machines deliver excellent signal to noise ratios, although you see fewer of them these days. A cassette deck with noise reduction circuitry (Dolby B, C, S, HX-PRO) will also make a fine tape. If using a cassette deck that does not have automatic bias control, try to match the tape bias to the deck's specs.
- Appropriate cables, extension chords, and high-quality recording tape

Figure 3.3 shows a typical recording setup. The most important part of making a basic tape, beyond the obvious points of keeping the room quiet and being prepared to give a good performance, is mike placement. Mike placement determines the amount of room ambience that will be on the tape, the timbre of the singer's voice, and quality of the diction. Some microphones (for example, single-D cardioids) exhibit bass proximity effect, that is, they get a bassier sound if you sing closer to them. This can add warmth to a recording if used carefully. Generally, the farther away the mike is from the sound source, the more room ambience and less detailed the sound (less diction). The two-position mike setup (Figure 3.3-A) allows some control of balance between the voice and piano since the mike pickup areas are well defined. Figure 3.3-B and C show two classic techniques for the use of directional microphones to create a stereo effect. Figure 3.3-B is the coincident-pair configuration, which produces a good stereo image when the performing group is small. Figure 3.3-C, the near-coincident-pair, produces a good stereo image with slightly better air than Figure 3.3-B.

The best continuous recording level for your tape is 0 VU. Because the piano and voice have a wide dynamic range that must be preserved, that level will only be attained during the loudest parts of the performance. Gain can be set in two ways. A friend could ride gain for you making sure to turn the volume down slowly when it exceeds 0 VU for too long. Or you could record your loudest section at several levels until you find the one that exceeds 0 VU only briefly and leave the levels set to that position for all of the recording.

Editing your tape is simply a matter of connecting your recording deck to another deck and recording your best takes onto another tape. The copying deck should be as good as the master deck. You will find that *slating* the cuts (announcing the number of the take and leaving five seconds of space before recording) will make your editing a lot easier.

If you are willing to experiment, you will discover that very good tapes can be made without having to rent costly studio time. For further information consult:

Bartlett, Bruce. *Introduction to Professional Recording Techniques.* Carmel, IN: Howard W. Sams & Co., 1987.

McIan, Peter. *The Musician's Guide to Home Recording.* New York: Simon and Schuster, 1988.

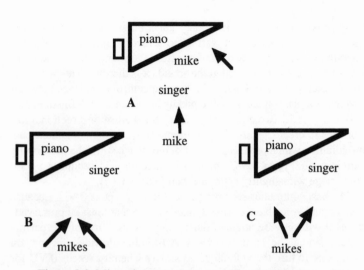

Figure 3.3. Microphone Arrangements for Amateur Recording

Portions of this section on Recording are from Richard Davis, "Making the Tape" *Journal of Singing* 52:2, 13-16. ©1996 by the National Association of Teachers of Singing, 2800 University Blvd. N., JU Station, Jacksonville, FL 32211. Used by permission.

Chapter 4

Vocal Ped-a-Who?

"Vocal ped-a-who?" was my daughter's response when I told her I was writing a book on vocal pedagogy. That kind of response is fairly common from the general public, so let's define our terms. Pedagogy is the art or profession of teaching. Vocal pedagogy is the art or profession of teaching voice. Pedagogy is also preparatory training or instruction. A growing number of colleges and universities offer voice pedagogy as a degree program (Cleveland, 1997). In these programs one learns how to teach singing by studying the writings of experts on voice teaching; learning how to interpret scientific research and perhaps doing some yourself; and teaching a student while under the supervision of an expert teacher. Many degree programs, other than those for voice pedagogy, have a voice pedagogy course requirement, most notably choral/vocal Bachelor of Music Education majors. It is for those students that this chapter and its companion chapter (For the Future Choral Conductor) are written.

Written voice pedagogy probably began with Caccini's (1545-1618) advice to singers about monody in *Le Nuove Musiche* (1602). It continued through the fabled teaching of the castrato Nicola Porpora (1686-1768) via his lost sheet of exercises, and continued into the eighteenth century with Tosi (1653-1732) (Tosi, 1743). Mathilda Marchesi (1821-1913) (Marchesi, 1901, 1903), who taught women in groups over a two year instruction period, and the Lampertis (Francesco Lamperti) (G. B. Lamperti in Brown, 1931) were the notables in the nineteenth century. The towering figure of the nineteenth century was Manuel Garcia, the son (1805-1906). In 1855 he invented the double mirror system of viewing the larynx that doctors use today. He rehabilitated the voice of Jenny Lind and was the teacher of Marchesi (Garcia, undated, 1849, 1894). It is with his work that scientific, as opposed to purely empirical, vocal pedagogy begins. Vocal pedagogy books, of both the scientific and empirical kind, have proliferated in the twentieth century. Seminal works by Sundberg, Appelman, Vennard, Richard Miller, and Titze have illuminated generations of those interested in the voice. A list of notable authors and scientific researchers can be found in the Selected Bibliography.

The field of vocal pedagogy, which began as advice to singers, has become increasingly dominated by hard science. It is a paradox that medical science—to which voice science is kin—usually debunks old accepted remedies, while voice science often gives proof to many of singing's traditional tenets. An example is Titze's explanation of vocal registers (1994, 252-277).

In today's world we are both bound and freed by science and technology. We are "living better through science," but we are also having to give up many things that make us human and unique. This is the case in today's vocal pedagogy. When science discovers what is valid in teaching methods, we feel obligated to use the validated methods and discard those that have no basis in fact. The discoveries narrow what we can present to the student, because we have fewer techniques from which to choose. In short, we give up a share of human tradition in favor of science.

Voice teachers have responded to scientific insight in two ways. The first response has been to ignore it altogether, saying, "If it's worked for three centuries and produced great singers it will work for my students." They rely on human tradition. Other voice teachers have tried to keep up their understanding of voice science. Their desire is to make up new methods based on the science they know, and apply old methods for the science they don't know. It is an eclectic method that favors science while keeping the connection to the human past. This eclectic system of teaching voice is growing in popularity, and it most likely will be a part of your learning.

Voice science is still an infant field of inquiry. It is based on interdisciplinary study. Professionals in health care, particularly otorhinolaryngologists, professionals in speech and hearing, and technically versed singing teachers, collaborate in over ninety-three speech labs across the country (Gould & Korovin, 1994). Their areas of inquiry are increasingly funded by grants in health care and college and university research.

Their findings over the past twenty-five years, which amount to
volumes of data, were mercifully summarized in an article by Thomas
Cleveland (1994). He reports the following as the most recent thoughts
in voice science.

1. The singer's formant is derived from a lowering of the
   larynx and widening of the laryngeal tube. It is not
   known whether articulatory adjustments may be used
   as well.
2. Vibrato is laryngeally based. Former respiratory theories are no long defensible.
3. Formant tracking has become the theory for explaining how and why vowels change with range. (See
   section on Resonation in Chapter 1).
4. Research on registers has shown that there is an interaction between the resonance of the trachea and the
   vocal folds that results in driving forces on the larynx
   that change its vibrational characteristics and produce
   registers. (Older theory was also based on vibrational
   changes in the folds but placed more emphasis on
   mechanical adduction as the cause of registers)
5. Subglottal pressure changes control the loudness of
   the voice, and the length of the folds controls the
   pitch. These parameters are not independent. Changes
   in pitch can be affected by subglottal pressure. Exercises that focus on changes in one parameter at a time
   (messa di voce) are beneficial, as are exercises that require the changing of both parameters (staccato exercises and arpeggii).
6. Timbre of the voice is determined by its formant frequencies, and the voice can be synthesized for experimentation.
7. Modes of phonation are located on a continuum from
   breathy (high airflow, glottis rarely closes) to flow
   (folds closed longer, wider glottis area, higher subglottal pressure, lower amplitude) to pressed (lower
   amplitude, high subglottal and adductory pressure,
   smaller glottal area).
8. Amateur singers use high laryngeal positions, and
   most classical singers use low laryngeal positions.

Some research has shown that tenors and some sopranos occasionally use high positions in the upper range, negating the bel canto theory that the larynx should always be low.

The discoveries of voice science are made through the use of the scientific method. A hypothesis is formulated and tested through a series of carefully planned experiments. In voice science the measurement of the results from those experiments is difficult, because much of the mechanism cannot be seen, and invasive protocols are frowned on by test subjects. Here is a list of some of the machines used for voice experimentation. Many are probably in the Speech and Hearing Department of your school, if it doesn't have a voice lab. The best reference for the strategies of measurement and the devices used to make those measurements is R. J. Baken's *Clinical Measurement of Speech and Voice* (1987). Many of the mechanisms documented have evolved to digital technology since the book was written. Reports on the latest developments can be found in the *Journal of Voice* (Gould & Korovin, 1994). Note that the following descriptions are intended as overview and that their brevity renders them incomplete.

- *Stroboscopic videolaryngoscope.* It allows stop-action video while photographing the vocal folds. It may be of the flexible or rigid tube type.
- *Computerized speech laboratory.* Kay Systems has an ever expanding program called *CSL.* (Mac Speech labs I and II are still found in many labs.) It provides pitch and amplitude (will measure jitter and shimmer), average DB, musical pitch correlation, long-term spectrum, spectrograms, cepstrum, fast fourier transform (FFT) measurement of formants, and linear predictive coding (LPC). The Kay program also has tools and games for the speech clinician.
- *Body plethysmograph.* A sort of steam cabinet-like box that when sealed can record thoracic volume displacements of the patient inside. Modified to record airflow.
- *Rothenberg mask.* A kind of pneumotachograph device for measuring airflow and air volume that with modifications can measure supraglottal pressure.

- *Magnetometers.* Hixon (1983) used these devices to measure movements of the abdomen and rib cage in seminal studies on breath management.
- *Nasometer.* Measures nasality via computer readout.
- *Oscilloscope.* Displays wave form generated from laryngograph.
- *Laryngograph.* Duration, velocity, and degree of vocal-fold closure during singing are represented in graphic format. Also called EGG (electroglottograph).
- *Kay Visi-pitch.* Older machine for making pitch assessments.
- *Spirometer.* Measures vital capacity by displacing water.
- *Ultrasound.* May develop into non-invasive technology for visualizing laryngeal function.
- *EMG.* Electromyography measures minute muscle contractions by inserting electrodes into the muscle. Very accurate measurements, but very invasive.
- *Computer programs* which combine the measurements of several different devices: GLIMPSES (glottal imaging by processing external signals) and ALBERT (acoustic and laryngeal biofeedback enhancement in real time).

Whether you choose to study the voice through scientific research or by reading the testaments of famous teachers and singers, you will always find it interesting. It is, after all, about the fascinating art of singing.

Chapter 5

For The Future Choral Conductor

Everyone who sings has been involved in a vocal ensemble of one kind or another. Some have been lucky enough to have deep emotional experiences while performing serious choral music with an eloquent and charismatic conductor. Others have enjoyed small ensembles that sang the gamut of vocal music from jazz to madrigals. Many singers have been so inspired by their group experience that they want to become choral directors, and American schools of music have accommodated that need by providing degree programs in choral education. It is for those singers that this chapter is written.

For some time now there has been an unfortunate polarization between solo singers and their teachers (soloists) on one hand and choral singers and their directors (choralists) on the other. The contentiousness between these two camps can manifest behavior patterns that can only be called comical. The solo singer takes the position that his instrument is to good to be lost in a crowd of singers, and the choral singer responds by accusing the solo singer of being too shallow and self-centered to be worthy of the choral experience. The soloist worries that his or her vocal technique will be lost for the sake of blend, and the choralist regards being able to blend the highest form of vocal technique. The voice teacher may appear to regard the choral director as a colleague while secretly steering students away from ensembles he or she regards as dangerous to the voice or too much of a time commitment. The choral director may indulge in the same duplicity by rewarding lesser singers in the choir with solos because they have good motivation toward choral music rather than the best voices. Arguments between choral directors and singing teachers are made more risible when you consider what they have in common. Choral directors are voice teachers. They work in a different medium but have as their common teaching goals the development of the voice, musical skills, and refinement of musical aesthetic. Regrettably, the contentions between choralists and soloists produce an atmosphere that stunts learning, diminishes credibility, and lowers everyone's perception of our art.

Many of the arguments between choralists and soloists result not from different goals but from the tyranny of different repertoires. The choral repertoire taught in universities goes all the way back to the roots of polyphonic music. The liturgical music of Josquin was performed in cathedrals that had a tendency to blur polyphonic textures. In order to clarify the texture, a vocal model was adopted that stressed rhythmic precision, relatively undifferentiated vowels, little dynamic change, well-blended tone, and relatively no vibrato. This stands in complete opposition the earliest solo vocal repertoire that is taught, namely bel canto. Agreement between soloists and choralists that all styles are valid and worthwhile would remove one of the sources of contention.

Another source of contention between soloists and choralists has to do with masterwork performance. Some large-scale works, such as the Bach *Mass in B-Minor* and all the symphonic choral works of Beethoven, make excessive demands on the tessitura and stamina of the young singer. Agreement between soloists and choralists that some works are out of bounds for the young singer would be helpful.

The last and most important contention between soloists and choralists has to do with "blend." I once heard Robert Shaw say that he didn't ever try to get one choral section to blend with another any more than he wanted the oboe to sound like the flute in the orchestra. He did get blend *within* each choral section by carefully choosing the the timbres of voices in the section. What was amazing is that he selected strong, well-produced, highly individual voices to produce his blend rather than altering the sound of every singer in the section. It was an example of balancing instead blending.

Many good books are available to the future choral conductor that outline everything from musical styles to electing choir officers (Collins, 1993; Robinson & Winold, 1992; Roe, 1994). A few points on voice building, warm-ups, choral techniques, and working with the immature voice warrant reinforcement here.

Because choral directors are voice teachers, time should be set aside in every rehearsal for voice building and vocal problem solving. The most popular place for this activity is during the vocal warm-up period.

A systematic approach to building the voice, combined with exercises formed from the difficult passages found in the choir's current repertoire, will go far beyond the mechanical repetition of some scales and arpeggii to get warmed up. The warm-up materials for the choir are an outgrowth of the vocalises found in Chapter 7, combined with some special techniques for working with groups. The warm-up can be divided up into the following areas of activity.

Physical Warm-up

Any physical exercise that will awaken the body and stimulate mental alertness can be used. Chair calisthenics, isometric exercise, stretching, jazz dance warm-ups, and partner massage can all be effective if changed every day.

Sensitize the Breathing Mechanism.
Some exercises are:
1. Deep diaphragmatic-intercostal breaths through mouth or nose with timed (1-5 second) inhalation and timed (5-10 second) exhalation. Exhalation can be hissed.
2. Flying. Raise arms with inhalation, lower arms without dropping chest as you slowly exhale through an open throat.
3. Panting. Make sure the pant is only on exhalation and that the diaphragm is moving up while pushing the air out.

Breath check
1. Place hands around the bottom of the ribs and check expansion during inhalation.
2. Place one hand on the epigastrium and one on the sternum. Watch both hands go out on inhalation. The epigastrium goes in on exhalation. Breath is replenished without dropping the chest by re-expanding at the level of the epigastrium.

Sensitize breath to tone connection (appoggio)
1. Short onset drills that stress soft attack, open fold releases, and a variety of vowels. (See breath exercise number 1.)

2. Messa di voce exercise and envelope-shaping exercises. (See register blending exercises in Chapter 7.) Make sure the *diminuendo* is not a *subito piano*.
3. Agility exercises. Scales and arpeggii at different speeds, vowels, and dynamic shapes. (See agility exercises in Chapter 7.)

Sensitize the Ear to Pitch and Vowel Timbre.

1. Tune and de-tune intervals. Ask the basses to sing a comfortably low note on [i]. Conductor sings the octave and slowly tunes the note sharp, then flat, then sings in tune. Choir listens for the beats. Expand the exercise to individuals in a section, then individuals in different sections, and then whole sections. Expand the drill using different intervals, vowels, and dynamics. Using chords in inversion and root position allow sections to tune and de-tune the chord.
2. Sing a chord progression by moving single notes like the exercise in Figure 5.1. This exercise is built on the omnibus progression. They are easily made by planing the top three voices up by half steps as the bass descends by half steps. For choral tuning exercises the omnibus is rhythmically broken down so that each voice moves alone.
3. Sing a chord progression in a common pattern like I-IV-V⁷-I, or from a piece you are performing, and ask the choir to silently sing one of the chords in the progression (pitch memory and tuning).
4. Drill scales and arpeggii highlighting vowel tracking from front to mid [i-a], mid to back [a-u], and then front to back through the intervening vowels [iɪeɛaɔouu]. Scales and arpeggii practiced on increasingly higher pitches have the added benefit of extending the range, provided the right vowel timbres are chosen by the conductor.
5. Sing a chord, flowing all the vowel sounds in a language through it. This can be particularly useful to unify the vowel timbres in a foreign language.
6. Brief articulation exercises that uncouple the move-

ment of the lips, jaw, and tongue from each other. On scales sing [bɛbɛ ...] while moving only the lips. Sing [lɑ lɑ ...] while moving only the tongue. Sing [jaja ...] while moving only the jaw.

Figure 5.1
Choral Tuning Exercise

Sensitize the Choir to the Conductor

Sensitize the choir to your conducting by changing tempo, mood, and style unexpectedly using only your hands and face. Make small gestures do all the work.

Solve vocal problems in your repertoire by making exercises out of them. If, for example, your sopranos are having difficulty singing [i] on an isolated high note (and who wouldn't?), build a scale exercise going above that note on [Ø]. Slowly substitute as much of the correct vowel timbre as you can into the exercise, and finally substitute the whole word after stopping on the pitch in the scale.

Vocal techniques and choral techniques are slightly different from each other because they are aimed at different populations and are devised by professionals with different interests. In addition to the warm-up exercises above and the vocal techniques provided in this book, here are some helpful choral techniques.

Agility

It does no good to practice melismatic passages by substituting nonsense syllables. It begs the question of agility by turning an agility exercise into a diction exercise. What does work is the pulsated drill. A continuous tone is articulated by light diaphragmatic pulses. Have the choristers sing a long note [a] while lightly pressing in on the epigastrium. Have them do it to quarters, duplets, triplets, and finally quadruplets in moderate time, letting the action come from the inside instead of the outside (no hands). Expand the single-note drill to scales and speed up the tempo.

Improving Tone

1. Describe the tone you seek as though you were writing a best-seller. Word pictures do translate into sound.
2. In order to get a high palate sound, have the choristers approach their mouth with their pointed index finger as they sing. Somehow the approaching finger raises the soft palate. It may hearken back to being fed as a child when Daddy told you, "Open the hangar, here comes the plane."

Dynamics

Diagram rehearsal of long crescendi and decrescendi over a specific number of beats (*p*, *mp*, etc.). Drill messa di voce stressing that the vowel should not change. Crescendi are made with tone, not just by opening the mouth. Practice the arch phrases on single vowels to highlight dynamic changes.

Balance

Shuffle arrangements can improve the balance of the sound and improve the weaker singers if you place them near the stronger ones. Singing in a circle always improves balance because singers are forced to listen for one another.

Posture

Think of a marionette with strings holding not only your spine straight, but your chest up as well.

Phrasing.
Ask the choir to mark the destination of each phrase in the score, and which line is the most important in the texture. Help them find the music among the notes.

Stage Presence
To explore the range of animation possible while singing, have the choir sing silently with their usual animation and ask them to add animation as the conductor "turns up the volume." Demonstrate what the song should look like as it is sung.

Order of Singing
Think the pitch. Think the vowel and the consonant. Inhale through the vowel space. Reverse the air's direction and sing.

Registration
Don't talk about it unless you have to. Hooting from the top down (siren) on different vowels will clear up all but the most entrenched problems. Serious problems, like tenors who cannot sustain the top voice or altos habitually in chest voice, will require sectionals and independent coaching.

Diction
Ask the choir to imitate British stage dialect when singing in English. Express vowel brightness and darkness as a continuum from 1 (very bright) to 10 (very dark) and ask for vowels by the numbers. "I want a 7 [a]." Diphthongs and triphthongs can be expressed on a continuum too. By giving the word a temporal value of 10, describe each phoneme as a numeric proportion of the sung word. For example, "say" is 9 for [e] and 1 for [i].
The efficacy of a choral technique is whether it works for you. Many techniques look great on the page, but may not get the same results when you use them. A great resource of succinct solutions for the ailing choir is *The Choral Conductor's Handbook* (Ehret 1959).

Developing the Young Voice

At the middle of this century very little was known about how voices mutated at puberty. Everyone knew that boys' and girls' voices darkened, that boys' ranges dropped about an octave, and that girls lost a few notes on the top. Thanks to the work of prominent educators in the field (McKenzie, 1956; Swanson, 1973; Barham & Nelson, 1991; Williams, Larson, & Price, 1996) and voice scientists (Cooksey, 1992), we are now more confident about having students continue to sing as their voices change. We also know that a majority of mutational disorders are caused by incomplete mutation (Brodnitz, 1983), that mostly boys are affected (falsetto remains as the speaking range), and that very few individuals are likely to have any postmutational problems. The majority of this work has been done on the male changing voice because of the dramatic nature of the voice change, but teachers working with girls must remember that their voices are also undergoing changes that require special care. A full discussion of this research is not possible here, but a summary of two very useful books and some comment on the commonality of training between boys' and girls' voices as they go through mutation will follow.

After careful studies, Cooksey (1992) has declared there are six stages of vocal change in the adolescent male from age ten to fifteen. Each of his stages notes age, lowering range and tessitura, change in timbre of the speaking and singing voice verified by acoustic analysis, physiological change, part assignment, and agility. As exhaustive as these categorizations are, he admits that the changing voice is a rule unto itself. While voices don't actually change overnight, some stages can be very short. Cooksey includes a very complete regimen for training young men's voices as they go through the change.

In *The Boy's Changing Voice* (Barham & Nelson, 1991) the authors reduce the categories of changing voice to four: treble, cambiata 1, cambiata 2, and baritone. The book deals with the whole experience of puberty. It offers useful advice on how to keep boys singing by promoting camaraderie and good self-image. It suggests useful musical materials and the Gordon tone syllable method. Like Cooksey, it contains notes on vocal technique for the changing voice.

A recurring theme in both books is that positive development of the adolescent voice depends on avoiding strain. It is necessary to audition changing voices regularly to assure that they are singing the right timbre, range, and tessitura.

Boys and girls going through puberty have many things in common. Their voices are changing at about the same time, age ten to fifteen, and their voices are changing in the same way. Ranges and tessitura are shifting downward and timbre is darkening. Both will lose high notes first and may experience thinning of sound, breathiness (which may continue a long while for girls), huskiness, and a general inconsistency of tone. Morphologically the same thing is happening to their larynges. They are becoming larger (the boys much larger) with the vocal bands increasing in length and thickness ahead of the musculature to control them. They are both experiencing register shifts, sometimes for the first time. They are both coping with an identity crisis caused by their changing bodies and changing social roles. They are both terrified of being made fun of or being out of place. Peers are very strong influences, and the desire to be cool is almost palpable. Within the context of these changes, vocal technique for both boys and girls must be focused on light, hummy production; maintaining good breath management; and exercising the whole of the range by blending registers downward. Musical materials must be carefully chosen to use only the notes easily available to the student and to motivate the student to keep singing.

Chapter 6

For the Future Teacher of Singing

Teachers of singing reflect the method by which they were taught to sing, the method they felt they learned (which is not always what they were taught!), the method they think their students should learn, and the way they studied teaching. On the basis of this diverse background they may classify their style of teaching as (1) bel canto; (2) psychological imagery; (3) scientific/mechanistic; or (4) eclectic.

The bel canto school flourished in Italy in the eighteenth century. Whether it arose as a technique for singing highly florid, wide-ranging melodies or whether composers wrote to exploit that technique we do not know. Either way, bel canto singers have been hailed as the greatest singers in the last three centuries. The three C's of bel canto are Caffarelli, Caruso, and Callas. The ideals of bel canto are a flowing legato, wide melodic and dynamic range, a broad palette of vocal colors leaning toward the bright side of the sound, equalized registers, flexibility, and a large, opulent tone. Some of the techniques and ideals of bel canto show up in every teaching method, no matter what it may be called.

The psychological imagery school of teaching shares the ideals of bel canto, but reaches them by using directives built upon suggestion and metaphor. It is a way of linking what psychology knows as the power of suggestion to the singing act. "Make a golden tone," "let the tone ride on the breath," and "feel the tone spin out to the audience" are examples of directives used in this style of teaching. Directives in this style of teaching are limited only to the imagination of the teacher.

The scientific/mechanistic school of teaching shares the ideals of bel canto, but relies on the discoveries of voice science as well as tradition for its logical, pragmatic directives. Directives are physical and usually observable. "Drop the jaw," "raise the soft palate," "pull the upper lip down," "don't tuck the chin," are examples of mechanistic directives. This type of directive is particularly effective when an observable behavior change needs to be made. It fails however, at transmitting concepts and musical ideas.

The eclectic school of teaching shares the ideals of bel canto, and is a pragmatic and variable response to the needs of the student. It recognizes the fact that no one approach will be right for every student and that the other three schools have strengths and weaknesses as educational methods. It requires that the teacher be schooled not only in traditional voice training, but science as well. The guiding principle of the eclectic teacher is find what works for the student and use it. The eclectic teacher is likely to use many physical directives (scientific/ mechanistic school) in the first part of study because behaviors like posture and breathing are observable. When trying to get a certain timbre from a student or build a concept of interpretation, the language of the psychological imagery school is effective. When establishing the aesthetics of singing, teachers often refer students to renowned bel canto singers as models.

It goes without saying that all of these styles of teaching can be supplemented by example. When words fail, an example is all that is left to get the idea across to the student. As a technique, teaching by example has some obvious flaws. The gender, voice type, and age of the teacher limit what can be believably demonstrated. A flawed demonstration usually leads to a flawed re-creation by the student.

Whatever system of directives the teacher uses, the backbone of instruction should be the basic skills observed in all professional educators. Planning the objectives for the student, initiating activities to reach those objectives, and evaluating progress are part of efficient instruction of any kind. In many cases this structure is not evident to the student but is being practiced on a subliminal level by the master teacher. As a beginning teacher you will have to make the discipline apparent to yourself and to your student to be successful.

To teach you must know how singers learn, and what intelligences must be stimulated. Howard Gardner, a noted educational theorist, has defined intelligence as "the capacity to solve problems or to fashion products that are valued in one or more cultural settings (Gardner & Hatch, 1989, 5)." He has further labeled music as one of seven basic intelligences (Gardner, 1983, 1993). Musical intelligence is characterized by interest, creativity, and skills in working with the core components of music. The core components are pitch, rhythm, timbre and the ability to perceive and manipulate form.

No one has just one intelligence, although most people seem to have one that is predominant and a family of others that support it (Krechevsky, 1991). People seem to be hard-wired at birth with a natural tendency to learn in a specific way and may be soft-wired, or taught to learn in other ways. For a singer, the ways in which they learn, or their most likely supporting intelligences, are linguistic (sound, rhythm, meaning of words), interpersonal (moods, temperament, motivations, desires of others), and intrapersonal (self-knowledge). Some very lucky singers also have bodily-kinesthetic intelligence (control of body movement and manipulation of objects). To simplify, singers are likely to know themselves and be adept with music, words, and feelings. They may also be able to move.

Once the singer's intelligences are assessed, the teacher can present activities that directly stimulate them. An older corollary to this rather complex idea can be found in "see, say, show." For example, a student makes a pitch error in a song he or she is singing. Some students will correct the error more quickly by looking at the music (see/visual learner). Some will respond more quickly by having the right pitch sung back to them (say/aural learner). Still others will correct it more quickly if they have a motion to associate with the phrase (show/kinesthetic learner).

Setting Student Goals

The first step in setting goals for the student is to know the student and find out what the student knows. Knowing the student is one of the most interesting parts of teaching. By conversation, whether oblique or direct, the teacher must learn why the student wants to sing, what kind of singing results in an emotional experience for him, what her level of dedication to singing is, what his work habits are, what she believes her level of talent is, what performance success has he known, and what her peripheral interests are. Using every *getting to know you* skill you have will pay dividends in understanding your student's needs and building the points of connection that lead to a trusting relationship. Finding out what the student knows is a little easier and can be accomplished by following a questionnaire (see the example in Chapter 7) and hearing him or her sing. A review of prior material studied (repertoire sheet), a review of performance experience, questions about key performance concepts, an agreement on the terms used to describe singing in the studio (nomenclature), questions about general health and fitness, and a description of the student's practice discipline are the minimum requirements for finding out what the student knows. The added bonus of preassessment is that it will eliminate re-teaching and its concomitant negative effect on a singer's motivation.

Goals work best when they are agreed upon by both the teacher and student. Such agreement implies that the student understands the goal and is motivated to achieve it. Goals should be attainable. A goal that cannot be attained frustrates the teacher and annuls the student's motivation. Goals should be constructed in a logical sequence of learning from easy to complex. As easy goals are attained the student is motivated to pursue more complex challenges.

Goals and objectives should have a behavioral basis. It is the student's singing performance—his or her behavior—that we are modeling. The cognitive domain (knowing the history of the composition) and the affective domain (evaluation of the song as an art work) are difficult to evaluate and are of importance mainly in the way they affect behavior. (For an explanation of educational domains, see Bloom 1956, 1964.)

John Mager in *Preparing Instructional Objectives* (1992) defines a method for stating behavioral objectives. The objective should contain three elements: (1) a statement of the observable behavior students are to perform as a result of instruction; (2) the conditions under which the behavior will be demonstrated; and (3) the criteria by which attainment of the objective will be judged. An example would be: Using a metronome set at 60 and rhythm syllables (the condition), the student will sing from letter A to B in Handel's *Oh, had I Jubal's Lyre* (the behavior) without losing the pulse or misnaming more than four syllables (the criteria). Goals like these are straightforward and because of their clarity inspire a measure of confidence in the process.

Activities

Devising activities to attain your students' goals is a creative enterprise. It goes without saying that technical progress is linked to the appropriateness of the music or vocalise selected for the student. Material with too many or too few challenges will stifle progress. Material that does not conform to a logical learning sequence will stifle progress. Material the student does not like or cannot establish an emotional connection to will stifle progress. Luckily, the voice teacher has great music from three and a half centuries to choose from!

The usual cycle of repertoire on the college level is based on the traditions of Western art music and proceeds roughly on a course of easy to difficult in terms of vocal technique, aesthetic understanding, and performance skill. The repertoire is defined not in terms of educational goals or competencies at certain times as much as it is by language. The first year concentrates on easy songs in Italian and English. The second year is dominated by German Lieder, spiced up with easy arias, and introduces the song cycle. The third year introduces the French melodie and more difficult arias and song cycles. The third year will culminate in a junior recital for performance majors. The fourth year is a putting-it-all-together year that ends in a senior recital displaying all of the areas of study.

Many feel that while this rather regimented system has served American education well, it may not be the right cycle of repertoire for everyone learning how to sing. Recent studies reconciling curriculum and the job offerings in the marketplace have caused the Eastman School of Music to revise its courses. With the concept of useful education in mind, voice teachers will increasingly follow a student's preferences for repertoire and activities.

Activities that help achieve a singer's goals are not always musical. Studying the life of the composer and poet, analyzing the poetry, studying performance techniques (acting), taking movement classes, and memorizing are examples of peripheral activities that are important to singing.

Evaluation

Evaluation carries the connotation of testing and will be replaced here with a more friendly term: feedback. Feedback is the third element of the teaching cycle behind goal setting and activity. It is very important that feedback be specific to the goal and activity. Nebulous comments like "that's nice" may make a student feel good, but they don't relate to a specific goal. If the student doesn't know if the goal has been accomplished how can he or she move on to the next goal in the sequence? Since learning to sing is cumulative, the successful steps have to be verified. Note that any musical activity may reflect more than one goal at a time, but it is difficult for the student to concentrate on more than one at a time. Nothing is more unnerving to the student than being asked to correct something, and then being stopped during the repetition for something else.

Feedback makes an activity memorable. When a student performs

an activity correctly, positive reinforcement will make it a part of his or
her long-term memory. Remembering success and forgetting failure is
part of the human psyche. Feedback, positive or negative, contains the motivation for repetition. It is for this reason that criticism must be specific and encourag-
ing in tone.

Closure at the end of the lesson is accomplished by summarizing
what goals have been accomplished and setting new goals for the practice room. One of the reasons for using the goal-activity-feedback form
of learning is that you want students to use it as they teach themselves
in the practice room.

Some Teaching Goals for the Teacher

Inspire your students. Your attitudes about the importance of music
in daily life, about the "flow" experience of performing, and about the
satisfaction that comes from knowing and doing new things will be
transferred to the student. Attitudes are caught, not taught. Students will
do what you do before they do what you say.

Teach for transfer. Learning is easier and more complete when integrated and associated with something already known. A vocalise that
the student has mastered can be applied to a like pattern in a song. The
study of European history can aid in understanding the life and times of
the great Western composers. The solfeggio taught in sight-singing
class is a more effective method for learning a difficult melody than
repetition.

Ask the right question and listen to the answer. Miscommunication
is the hallmark of failed relationships. Communication is a loop. A
says something, B hears it, and if B understands it, acknowledges to A
that the message has been received. If either A or B does not listen, no
message is communicated. Voice teachers should talk during the lesson
less than the student does. Asking closed- and open-ended questions during the lesson and listening to the response will tell you what the student knows and lead her to discovering what you want her to know. Discovery is a stronger teaching method than lecturing. Some examples of
open-ended discovery questions are:

• Why do you suppose that phrase ends on that chord?
• What do you like about the character the poet has
  created?

Some examples of closed-ended questions are:

- Where is the destination of this phrase?
- How do you pronounce "h-e-u-t-e"?

Listen for subtext. What a student says may be miles away from what he means. Salespeople always say that the highest compliment you can pay to clients is to listen to them with concentration. That can be said about the teacher-student relationship too.

Connect the dots. Knowledge is acquired in small bits that in themselves are useless and unmemorable unless they can be strung into a concept. A rule, a generalization, a conclusion, or a concept made from many experiences and facts will transfer to a new situation and be memorable. Just as it is better to teach a poor man to grow corn than it is to give it to him, so is it better to teach a student the rules of German pronunciation than have her mimic gibberish.

Reading beyond the sources mentioned in this chapter might include Maslow's hierarchy of needs, Piaget's theories of cognitive development, and Erickson's theories of psychosocial development.

Chapter 7

Singer's Tool Kit

This chapter is a collection of useful information for the voice teacher, the future voice teacher, and the voice student. It contains materials for daily use: diction guides, a list of songbooks for the young singer, a list of vendors, a study guide for songs and this text, a questionnaire for new students, a practice log, a sample jury sheet, and vocalises.

The International
Phonetic Alphabet (IPA)

The IPA is based upon the idea that all the phonemes in all the languages can be reduced to a single set of characters. Those characters can then be used to write the sounds of all the languages. Its advantage to the student learning foreign languages is universality. Once the symbols are learned you can convert a transcription in IPA into the singing of a song in a foreign language, even though you are not a master of that language. *There is no substitute for fluency in a foreign language.* There are slight variations in the pronunciation of the phonemes called allophones that will mark a non-native singer as foreign to the native listener. Local dialectal differences can further separate the non-native singer from the native-speaking audience. IPA is an expedient, one that must be observed in the compressed college curriculum. The most familiar IPA symbols are given here in a correlative way, with words in English, German, Italian, and French used as models. The convention for writing in IPA is to enclose the phonemes in brackets. In these charts the phoneme relates to the italicized letters of the foreign word.

IPA	ENGLISH	GERMAN	ITALIAN	FRENCH
[i]	seen	Lied	si	fille
[I]	fin	ich	—	—
[e]	chaos	mehr	pena	enchantée
[ɛ]	bet	Bett	tempo	père
[ae]	sat	—	—	—
[a]	lamb	—	—	parle
[ɑ]	father	Fach	fatale	âge
[ɔ]	all	Sonne	morta	somme
[o]	note	Sohn	non	pauvre
[ʊ]	foot	Mutter	—	—
[u]	fool	Ruhe	uso	ou
[ʌ]	up	—	—	—
[ə]	ahead	gesund	—	demain
[y]	—	müde	—	une
[Y]	—	Glück	—	—
[ø]	—	schön	—	peu
[œ]	—	können	—	heure

Nasals

[ã]	—	—	—	temps
[ɛ̃]	—	—	—	vin
[õ]	—	—	—	non
[œ̃]	—	—	—	parfum

Semivowels

| [j] | yes | ja | piu | hier |
| [w] | wish | — | uomo | moins |

IPA	ENGLISH	GERMAN	ITALIAN	FRENCH

Diphthongs

IPA	ENGLISH	GERMAN	ITALIAN	FRENCH
[aɪ]	n*i*ce	—	—	—
[ɑe]	—	M*ai*	—	—
[ɑi]	—	—	m*ai*	—
[aU]	ho*u*se	—	—	—
[ɑo]	—	H*au*s	—	—
[ɑu]	—	—	*au*ra	—
[eI]	w*ay*	—	—	—
[ei]	—	—	dov*ei*	—
[ɔI]	b*oy*	—	—	—
[ɔø]	—	H*äu*ser	—	—
[ɔi]	—	—	vu*oi*	—
[oU]	s*o*	—	—	—

Consonants

IPA	ENGLISH	GERMAN	ITALIAN	FRENCH
[θ]	*th*ink	—	—	—
[ð]	*th*e	—	—	—
[ç]	—	i*ch*	—	—
[x]	—	a*ch*	—	—
[ɲ]	o*n*ion	—	so*gn*o	Ai*gn*er
[ŋ]	so*ng*	—	—	—
[r]	ve*r*y (single tap, repeated for pre-roll exer. ve*r*y, me*rr*y etc.)			
[r:r]	—	knu*rr*en (rolled r)	te*rr*a	—
[ʃ]	*sh*op	—	—	—
[ʒ]	vi*s*ion	—	—	—
[tʃ]	*ch*ase	Ki*tsch*	*ci*elo	—
[dʒ]	ju*dg*ment	—	*gi*urare	—
[ts]	*ts*e*ts*e	Zauber	*z*io	—
[dz]	a*dd*s	—	*z*ero	—
[ʌ]	—	—	fo*gl*ia	—

Language Pronunciation Guides

Not so many years ago, before the popularity of the IPA, oleographic guides were the resource for beginners singing in foreign languages. Knowing the IPA is helpful when reading someone else's transcription of a song, or as a mnemonic device for recording the vowel prescription of your teacher, but it doesn't acquaint you with *which letters* represent *which sounds* when you are a novice reader. The following guides are certainly not exhaustive. It is assumed that the student of singing will eventually take diction and foreign language classes. In the meantime, these simple guides will serve as a starting point for the beginner.

Italian

The Italian language is very fluid, that is, one word flows continuously into the next with very little interruption. This is the reason it is so often chosen as the beginning language for the singer. It is easy to pronounce. A common error for non-native singers is adding a vowel to make a diphthong where a pure vowel should be sung. This is a particular problem in words that end in a vowel. Only the vowels written are to be pronounced. There is very often some question as to whether a specific incidence of *e* or *o* should be open or closed. A good Italian dictionary can give guidance on the opening and closing of stressed *e* or *o*. Consonants not listed are pronounced much like those in English. The overarching concept in Italian pronunciation is to keep the sounds "close to the teeth."

Vowels

Italian	IPA	Italian	IPA	Italian	IPA
a	[ɑ]	e	[e]	e	[ɛ]
i	[i]*	o	[o]	o	[ɔ]
u	[u]**				

* Also pronounced as [j] when preceding a stressed vowel or between two vowels; sometimes silent serving as a marker to soften *c*, *g*, and *sc*, e.g., *già*.
** Also pronounced as [w] when followed by a stressed vowel, e.g., *questo*.

Consonants

c [k] before a, o, and u or consonants; [tʃ] before e and i
ch [k] before e and i
d [d] dental
g [g] before a, o, and u or consonants; [dʒ] before e and i
gh [g]before e or i
gli [ʎ] within a word; [ʎi] gli as a word or at the end of a word
gn [ɲ]
h is silent, added to harden g before e or i, e.g. *laghi*
l [l] dental
n [n] dental
r [r] flipped between vowels; rolled in all other positions
rr [rːr]
s [z] between vowels or before a voiced consonant in the same word; [s]
    in all other places.
sc [sk] before a, o, and u and consonants; [ʃ] before e or i
sch [sk] before i or e
t-[t] dental
z-consult a dictionary to determine if it is [ts] or [dz]
zz-consult a dictionary to determine if it is [tts] or [ddz]

In monosyllables beginning with *ci, gi,* and *sci* followed by *a, o,* or *u,* the *i* is silent. When the stress falls on the *i* the combination becomes a diphthong. Examples are *mio, Dio,* and *sia*. Vowels spelled with accents are always stressed. In any diphthong or triphthong one of the vowels will be stressed, that is, held longer than the other vowels. Double consonants are three times as long as single consonants and may employ a stop if sung dramatically.

Spanish

Spanish song pronunciation should correspond to the regional dialect of the poetry or to the Spanish spoken by the composer. Hence we hear Andalusian, Catalonian, Castilian, and Latin American Spanish from authentic Spanish singers. In general, use Castilian for composers from Spain and Latin American Spanish for those from the Americas. Of all the Romance languages, Spanish is the most phonetic. Modern Spanish is recommended for those unfamiliar with dialect.

There is a tendency in Spanish, as there is in Latin and Italian, for English singers to add vowels sounds, particularly to final *e* and *o*, making diphthongs where none are found. This is to be avoided. Some sources list brighter and more open vowel sounds than you will find here, [ɛ] [ɔ]. As always, there is no substitute for fluency in a foreign language to be truly authentic.

Vowels
a [a]
e [e]
i [i] when the only vowel in the syllable, or when in combination with other vowels and stressed (spelled with an accent mark); [j] unstressed, when preceding or following a, e, o, or u in the same word
o [o]
u [u] when the only vowel in the syllable
u [w] unstressed, when preceding a, e, i, o, or y in the same word
    u is silent in gue, gui, unless the u is spelled with a dieresis, silent in que, qui
y [i] when final in ay, ey, oy, and uy combinations
y [j] in other cases

Consonants
b [b]
c [k] before a,o,u or consonants (except h)
c [s] before e or i (Latin American)
c [ø] before e or i (Castillian)
cc [ks]
ch [t]
d [d] dental
f [f]
g [g] before a, o u, or consonants
g [h] before e or i (Latin America)
g [x] before e or i (Castillian)
h -silent
j [h] (Latin America)
j [x] (Castillian)
k [k]
l [l]
ll [j] (Latin American)

ll [ʎ] (Castillian)
m [m]
n [n] in many cases
n ñ [ŋ] before [g] and [k] sounds, regardless of spelling
p [p]
q [k]
r [r] flipped
rr [r:r] rolled
s [s] in most cases; [z] before voiced consonants, even when the voiced
    consonant is in the next word
t [t]
v [b] sometimes heard as halfway between [b] and [v].
w [w]
x [s] initial; [ks] internal
z [s] (Latin America); z [θ] (Castillian)

Latin

Latin pronunciation varies by country. German choirs use ecclesiastical Latin, which sounds different from the Latin heard in the Roman Church. Roman Latin is most often used in America because it is more familiar to those Americans who can remember what the Latin Mass sounded like when it was intoned in churches in the first half of the twentieth century. Latin, like Italian, often suffers from diphthonging, that is, adding vowel sounds where none is written. This is most likely to occur on final vowels. Latin may suffer from careless substitutions as well: [ə] for unstressed [ɑ], [e] for [ɛ], [ɪ] for [i], and [ʊ]for [u]. Double vowels require a re-energizing of the sound after a gentle separation, e.g., *filii*. A dieresis means vowels should be pronounced separately, e.g., *Michaël*. Double consonants are slightly sustained. Consonants not listed are pronounced much like English.

Vowels

Latin	IPA	Latin	IPA	Latin	IPA
a	[ɑ]	e	[e]	æ	[ɛ]
œ	[ɛ]	i	[i]	i*	[j]
o	[ɔ]	u	[u]	u**	[w]
y	[i]				

* Intervocalic as in cuius.
** When preceded by q or ng and followed by a vowel as in qui.

Diphthongs

Latin	IPA	Latin	IPA
au	[ɑu]	ai	[ɑi]
ae,oe	[ɛ]		

Consonants

c [tʃ] before e, i, y , ae , oe; [k] before a,o,u, or a consonant e.g.,
    Christ

cc [ttʃ] before e, i, y, ae, oe; [kk] before a, o, u or a consonant

g [dʒ] before e, i, y, ae, oe; [g] before a,o,u or consonants

gn [ɲ] ; [gn] when initial in a word e.g. gnarus

h is silent; [k] in two words mihi and nihil

j [j]

ph [f]

qu [kw]

r [r]

rr [r:r]

s-[s]; [z] between two vowels. Note that eccle-
    siastical Latin maintains s is always [s] not [z].

sc-[ʃ] before e, i, y, ae, oe; [sk] in all other places

ti [tsi] when followed by a vowel and preceded by any letter except s, t,
    or x; e.g., etiam

ti [ti] e.g. timor

th [t]

x [gz] when followed by a vowel or an h and in initial ex; e.g., exaudi,
    exultate; [kʃ] when initial exc followed by e, i, y, ae, or oe; e.g.,
    excelsis; x [gz] when initial in exs followed by a vowel; e.g., ex-
    sultate; x [ks] when initial in exs followed by a consonant; e.g. ex-
    specto; x [ks] in all other cases; e.g. pax, lux, dixit, resurrexit

v [v]

z [dz] e.g. Lazarus, Nazareth.

French

The French language is considered by some to be the most lyric of all the Romance languages because of its connections between words and its lack of consonant stops. The connectivity of the language is enhanced by two customs of pronunciation: liaison and elision. Liaison occurs when a usually silent final consonant is pronounced before a vowel initial or initial mute *h* (e.g., *les hommes*). Liaison varies with text styles, the place it is being read, and the heritage of the speaker. Folk texts are less likely to have liaison than more formal texts used in singing. Regardless of how much liaison is used, textual intelligibility must be preserved. Liaison can make very strange meanings—*trop-homme de terre* becomes *pomme de terre* in the same way that "let us pray" can become "let us spray."

Most diction books, including Bernac and Grubb, contain a long list of rules by which liaison is determined by parts of speech. In general, while singing art songs, oratorio, and opera, use liaison liberally, as long as the rules that forbid it are adhered to and the meaning of the words is not distorted.

Determining where liaisons should occur is much more complicated than applying elision. Elision is the omission of the final mute e so that the final sounded consonant links to the next word when that word begins with a vowel, a semivowel, or a mute *h* (e.g., *notre amour*).

Elision and liaison are processes that reflect the ideals of French lyric diction: every syllable should contain only one vowel; every syllable should begin with a consonant and end with a vowel; vowels should be long and consonants short with only limited stress and continuous tone throughout the vocal line.

The complete rules for pronouncing French lyric diction are complicated, lengthy, and too numerous to list here. Studying French and listening to French singers is a more satisfying way to get an ear for the language than memorizing rules, but few students have time to do a thorough study of French before singing their first French song! The rules which follow form the simplified basis of French lyric diction.

Liaisons are *forbidden*:
- Between two words that are not closely related in meaning (a comma separates these words in many cases)
- Over a musical rest or a breath in the vocal phrase
- Before the word *oui*

- After a singular noun
- After a proper name
- After the conjunction *et*
- Before the numbers *un, huit,* and *onze*
- Before an aspirate *h*

A special case: in words that end with *rt, rd, rs,* sound the *r* in liaison rather than the final written consonant, except when the *s* indicates a plural, then sound the *s* in liaison

In French diction final consonants are usually silent, with final *e* usually sung as [ə]. French pronunciation is filled with exceptions to the rules. Further information is available in Grubb.

Vowels

a [a] although the phoneme [ɑ] is proper in a few cases it is disappearing in modern French, particularly among the younger generations

à [a]

â [a]

ai[ɛ] most of the time; [e] when final in a word; [ə] in the words faisons, faisais, and faisant

aie [ɛ]

aient [ɛ]

ail, aill [aj]; [ɛl] when not final.

aim, ain [ɛ̃]; [ɛ] when immediately followed by a vowel, m, or n in the same word (the second m or n would be sounded)

ais [ɛ]

ait [ɛ]

am, an [ɑ̃]; [a] when immediately followed by a vowel, m, or n in the same word (the second m or n would be sounded)

au [o]; [ɔ] when followed by r

ay [ej]; [ɛi] in the word pays and its derivatives

e [ə] at the end of a syllable or a word if the e is assigned a note in the music (including polysyllabic words ending in -es when the -es indicates a plural). If not assigned a note the e is silent. [ə] in

French is slightly lip rounded.

e [e] when followed by final, silent d, ds, r or z and in the words et, eh, and clef

e [ε] when followed by a sounded consonant at the end of the syllable,
  when followed by silent t at the end of a word (except the word et), and in the word est. *See exceptions below.*

e [a] irregularly in the words femme, solennel, ardemment, and fréquement.

e between [e] and [ε] in the words les, des, ces, mes, ses, and tes.

é [e]

ê [ε]

è [ε]

eau [o]

eff, ess, desc, dess [e], when these spellings are initial in a word

ei [ε] except when followed by l, m, or n. *See below.*

eil, eill [εj]

eim, ein [ɛ̃]; [ε] when followed by a vowel, m, or n in the
  same word (the second m or n would be sounded)

em, en [ɑ̃]; [a] when followed by a vowel, m, or n in the
  same word (the second m or n would be sounded)

ent [ə] in a third-person plural verb ending

eoi [wa] silent e

eu [œ] when followed by a pronounced consonant in the same word,
  except the [z] sound

eu [ø] when final sound in a word (not necessarily the final spelling);
  when immediately followed by the [z] sound in the same word

eu [y] in the conjugation of avoir (to have)

euil, euill [œj].

ey [εj]

i [i] when final or before a consonant in the same word, except when
  nasal

i [j] before a stressed vowel, except when the i is assigned a note (or is
  otherwise marked to be sung in a separate syllable). In this case i is
  pronounced [i]

ï [i]

ie [jɛ] when followed by a sounded consonant at the end of the syllable

ie [je] when followed by a silent consonant at the end of the syllable, other than rn or n

ien [jẽ] except in the groups listed below

ience, ient [iɑ̃] when final, in words other than verbs

ient [i] third-person plural verb ending when assigned one note (or otherwise marked to be sung in one musical motive)

ient [iə] third-person plural verb ending when assigned two notes (or is otherwise marked to be sung in two syllables)

ie [i] when final and assigned one note (or otherwise marked to be sung in one musical motive). This includes ies (second-person singular verb ending and nouns).

ie [iə] when final and assigned two notes (or is otherwise marked to be sung in two syllable). This includes ies (second person singular verb ending and nouns).

iè [jɛ] when assigned one note

iè [iɛ] when assigned two notes (or otherwise marked to be sung in two syllables)

ieu [jø] when final sound in a word (not necessarily the final spelling) or when immediatley followed by the [z] sound in the same word, *and* when assigned one note (or otherwise marked to be sung in one musical motive)

ieu [iø] when final sound in a word (not necessarily the final spelling) or when immediately followed by the [z] sound in the same word, *and* when assigned two notes (or otherwise marked to be sung in two syllables)

ieu [jœ] when followed by a pronounced consonant in the same word, except the [z] sound *and* when assigned two notes (or otherwise marked to be sung in two syllables)

il [j] when final and preceded by a vowel

il [il] when initial

ill [j] when medial and preceded by a vowel

ill [ij] when not preceded by a vowel, except in the words mille, ville, and tranquille (and a few less common words), and their derivatives. In these words the group is pronounced [il].

im, in [ɛ̃]; [i] when followed by a vowel m, n, or h in the same word
    (the second m or n would be sounded)
o [ɔ] except as listed below.
o [o] when final sound in a word (not necessarily the final spelling);
    when immediately followed by a [z] sound in the same word; when
    followed by -tion
ô [o]
oeil, oeill [œj]
oeu [œ] when followed by a pronounced consonant in the same word
oeu [ø] when final sound in a word (not necessarily the final spelling)
oi [wa] except when nasal; see below
oin [wɛ̃]; [wan] when followed by a vowel in the same word.
om, on [õ]; [ɔ], when followed by a vowel, m, n, or h in the
    same word (the second m or n would be sounded)
ou [u]
où [u]
oû [u]
ouill, ouill [uj]
oy [waj]
u [y] except before a stressed vowel in the same word. In this case it is
    pronounced [ɥ]; if the u and the stresssed vowel are assigned two
    notes (or otherwise marked to be sung in two syllables) the u is
    pronounced [y]. u is silent when preceded by g and followed by a
    vowel and silent when preceded by q (there are a few exceptions to
    both cases; check a dictionary that includes IPA symbols).
û [y]
ueil, ueill [œj]
um, un [œ̃]; [y] when followed by a vowel, m, or n in the
    same word (the second m or n would be sounded)
uya [ɥija]; [ɥijɑ̃] when nasal
uya [yjɑ̃] when preceded by a consonant followed by l or r and when the
    group is followed by n.
uye [ɥije]; [ɥiə] when the word ends -ent, indicating a third-person
    plural verb
y [i]; [j] when initial and followed by a vowel; [ij] when intervocalic.

The [i] conjoins with the preceding vowel; the [j] conjoins with
the following vowel to form letter groups for the sake of pronunciation.

ym, yn [ɛ̃]; [i] when followed by a vowel, m, or n in the
same word (the second m or n would be sounded)

Consonants

b [b]; [p] when followed by an unvoiced consonant; silent when final
and preceded by a nasal vowel

c [k] when followed by a, o, u, or a consonant (except ch, in most
cases); when final (in most words); [s] when followed by e, i, or y;
silent when final and following a nasal vowel

ç [s]

cc [k] when followed by a, o, u, or a consonant

cc [ks] when followed by e, i, or y

ch [ʃ]; [k] in most words of Greek origin (Christ, orchestre, écho,
choeur)

cqu [k]

ct [kt] or silent; check a dictionary which includes IPA symbols

d [d] ;silent when final, except the word sud, and in some proper names.
This includes final ds when the s indicates a plural, and in some
verbs.

d [t] when sounded in liaison

f [f] except when sounded in liaison

f [v] when sounded in liaison

g [g] when followed by a, o, u, or a consonant (except n)

g [ʒ] when followed by e, i, or y

g [k] when sounded in liaison

g is silent when final

gg [g] before a, or, u, or a consonant

gg [gʒ] before e, i, or y

gn [ɲ]

gs is silent when final and following a nasal vowel

gt is silent when final

h is silent

j [ʒ]

k [k]

l [l]; silent in gentil, and when final in a few other words. The word fils

is a special case. When it means "son" it is pronounced [fis]; when
it means "thread" or "filament" it is pronounced [fil]

l [j] in final ail, eil, euil, and ouil

ll [j] in most words, especially the groups aill, eill, euill, and ouill.
Exceptions are words beginning with ill, and the words mille,
ville, tranquille, and their derivatives. In these cases the group is
pronounced [il].

m [m]; silent when serving to indicate a nasal vowel, except when
sounded in liaison. Also silent in the words automne and damner

n [n]; silent when final

p [p]; silent when final

ph [f]

pt [pt] or [t]; check a dictionary which includes IPA symbols

q [k]

r [r]; silent in most polysyllabic words ending in er (including final ers
when the s indicates a plural), except in the words enfer, hiver,
cuiller, amer, and a few less common words

s [z] when intervocalic or sounded in liaison

s is silent when final, except in a few words and in most proper names,
including lys, hélas, jadis, meurs, sens, fils (meaning thread), iris,
Francis, Reims, Mars, Damis, Tirsis, Bilitis, Saint-Saëns)

t [t]; silent when final, except in a few words, including sept, huit, di
-rect, correct, eat, ouest, soit, Christ; [s] when followed by i pro
nounced [j]. The most common spellings are final -tion and -tience.
An exception is final -tion preceded by s. In this case t is pro
nounced [t].

th [t]

v [v]

w [v]

x [s]; [ks] when followed by a consonant; [gz] when followed by a
vowel or h in the same word, except in numbers; silent when final,
except in numbers, or when sounded in liaison, or in a few words
including index, Casix; [z] when sounded in liaison in the words
deuxième, sixième, and dixième; [s] in the numbers six, dix, and
soixante

z [z]; silent when final, except in proper names, such as Berlioz and
Boulez

German

German, like English is aphonetic, that is, spelling does not always follow the sound of the phonemes. German is generally thought of as a guttural language; however, most lyric German singing does not have a guttural sound even though it does have many consonant stops. The rounded frontals in German, like those of French, are the most difficult for English-language speakers. Drills found in the vocalise section will help to develop the correct timbres.

Vowels

a [ɑ]

ä [e] when followed by an h in the same word, or by only a single consonant

ä [ɛ] when followed by more than one consonant *

e [e] when followed by an h in the same word, or by only one consonant, or when doubled. In high German this vowel has more [i] blended into it than we expect.

e [ɛ] when followed by more than one consonant,* and in the prefixes er-, ent-, emp-, her-, ver-, weg-, and zer-

e [ə] when unstressed and in the prefixes ge- and be-

i [i] when followed by an h in the same word, or by a single consonant; [I] when followed by more than one consonant.*

o [o] when followed by an h in the same word, or by only one consonant, or when doubled or final in a word; e.g., ohne, Boot, also; [ɔ] when followed by more than one consonant*

ö [ø] when followed by an h in the same word, or by a single consonant; [œ] when followed by more than one consonant*

u [u] when followed by an h in the same word, by a single consonant or final; [ʊ] when followed by more than one consonant

ü [y] when followed by an h in the same word, or by a single consonant; [ʏ] when followed by more than one consonant*

y [y] when followed by a single consonant; [ʏ] when followed more than one consonant*

* The basic rule in German is that a vowel followed by more than one

consonant is more open than when followed by *h* or a single consonant. There are exceptions to this vowel-opening rule that can be confirmed by the dictionary.

Diphthongs

ai, ay, ei, ey [ɑe]

au [ɑo]

ie [i]

eu, äu [ɔɪ]

Consonants

b [b]; [p] when final in a word, prefix, or word root. e.g., ob, ablegen, liebchen

c   appears in words borrowed from other languages.

ch [ç] after i,e, and ie; [x] after a,o,u, au (except eu and äu diphthongs)

ch [k] in words of Greek origin e.g., Orchester, Christ

chs [ks] when s is part of the root word e.g., sechs

ck [kk] as if double consonant, sustained in singing

d [d] initial and middle; [t] final

f [f]

g [g] initial or middle; [k] final [k] e.g.,Tag

ig [ɪç] when final or in a word root

ig [ɪk] when followed by the suffixes -lich or -reich e.g., ewiglich

h [h] when initial and in the suffixes -heit and -haft. Silent in other places

j [j]

k [k]

l [l]

m [m]

n [n] usually. Exceptions include some ng and nk combinations.

ng [ŋ] when the letters are in the same word root or suffix e.g. singen, Angst

ng [ng] when the letters are in different word elements and part of a prefix or the first part of a compound word e.g., hingehen, Ungeduld

nk [ŋk] when in the root word

nk [nk] in other cases

p [p]
ph [f]
qu [kv]
r [r] usually flipped in singing. One may choose to substitute the open
    [ə] in the following four cases: in short words such as "der;" in
    prefixes that end in r, such as er-, ver-, and vor-; in unstressed er
    when it is final in a word or root word such as Singer; and un-
    stressed er when it occurs before a final consonant in words
    such as wandern.

Note that flipping and rolling r have been historically been a matter of
taste. The custom changes with the time. A singer who rolls every r
would be regarded as affected today, but in the past, this was regarded as
perfect diction.

rr [r:r]
s [z] before a vowel; [s] in all other cases
sch [ʃ]
sp [ʃp] when initial in a word or root word; [sp] in other cases

st [ʃt] when initial in a word or word root; [st] in other cases.
t [t]
v [f]; [v] in some words of foreign origin, such as Rosenkavalier
    and Klavier
w [v]
x [ks]
z [ts]

German has some unique features: the nouns are capitalized, double
consonants are sustained during singing, and the letter ß is used in older
writing and represents ss. Correct pronunciation often depends on dis-
tinguishing the root words from prefixes, suffixes, and verb and adjective endings. Here are some examples of nonroot combinations.

Common German Prefixes

ab	an	auf	aus	be	bei	da	dar
durch	ein	ent	er	fort	ge	her	hin
miss	mit	nach	über	um	un	unter	ur
ver	vor	weg	zer	zu			

Common German Suffixes

bar	chen	haft	heit	ig	ige	in	keit
lein	lich	ling	los	nis	sal	sam	schaft
tum	ung	voll	wärts				

Common Verb and Adjective Endings

e	en	est	et	ste	t	ten	te
test	tet						

Practicing Rounded Frontal Vowels

Singing in French and German requires singers to accurately produce vowel sounds that are not found in English. Americans sometimes believe, because the rounded frontals are difficult, that learning just one will be enough to get by in the language. True phonemic accuracy demands that all of the rounded frontals be mastered. The best way to build skills in these sounds is to practice them in discrimination drills. Compare the rounded frontals by singing them in the exercise below. (sequentially from bright to dark vowels, one per exercise) Here are some words with those sounds to help you remember the differences.

[y] built on [i] plus [u]: Gr. kühl, für, über; Fr. du, murmure, une

[ʏ] built on [I] plus [ʊ]: Gr. hübsch, geküsst, lüfte

[ø] built on [e] plus [o]: Gr. böse, höh, Vögel; Fr. Dieux, heureux, radieuse

[œ] built on [ɛ]plus [ɔ]: Gr. öffen, möchte, lösche; Fr. coeur, pleur, jeune

[y ʏ ø œ]

Repertoire for the Young Singer

As a matter of economy and convenience, most of the song assignments made during the first years of study come from collections of
songs rather than single sheets. Many times, because of the universal
appeal of these collections, it may be possible to pool your resources
with your fellow students and have access to many collections. Below
are listed some of the studio favorites with approximate prices.

Actor's Songbook. Men's and women's editions, Hal Leonard. $19.95.

Album of 25 Songs for Girls. G. Schirmer. $16.95.

*Anthology of Italian Songs of the Seventeenth and Eighteenth Centu-
ries.* Book 1, Alessandro Parisotti, ed., G. Shirmer. $9.95.

L'Aria Barocca. John Glenn Paton, ed., Leyerle Pub.

The Art Song. Alice Howland and Poldi Zeitlin, eds., Consolidated
Music Pub.

Art Songs for School and Studio. Mabelle Glenn and Alfred Spouse,
eds., first and second year. Each volume in medium high and medium
low. Oliver Ditson Pub. $6.50-7.95.

Basic Repertoire for Singers. Robert W. Ottman and Paul G. Krueger,
eds., Southern Music Pub. $5.00.

Best of Pathways of Song. Laforge/Earhart eds., low and high, Warner
Bros. $10.95.

Classical Contest Solos. soprano, mezzo-soprano, tenor, baritone/bass,
CD included, Hal Leonard. $15.95.

Fifty-seven Classic Period Songs. Van Christy, ed., medium high and
medium low, Belwin Mills. $12.50-22.00.

*The First Book of [Soprano, Mezzo-Soprano, Tenor, Baritone/Bass]
Solos.* Compiled by Joan Boytim, available in Part I and Part II, CD
available, Hal Leonard Pub. $10.95.

Five Folk Songs. arr. L. Zaninelli, high, medium, Shawnee Press.

Five Shakespeare Songs. Roger Quilter, second set, high, low, Boosey and Hawkes.

Folksong Arrangements. Benjamin Britten, six volumes, high, medium, Boosey and Hawkes.

Folksongs for Solo Singers. Jay Althouse, ed., medium high and medium low, with or without cassette, Alfred Publishing.

Heritage of Twentieth Century British Song. four volumes, medium, Boosey and Hawkes. $14.00.

Imperial Edition. Sydney Northcote, ed., soprano, mezzo, contralto, tenor, baritone, bass songs, Boosey and Hawkes. $14.00.

Italian Songs of the Eighteenth Century. Albert Fuchs, ed., International Music Co. $9.00.

Italian Songs of the Seventeenth and Eighteenth Centuries. L. Dallapiccola, ed., two volumes, each available in high, medium and low, International Music Co. $8.00.

Old American Songs. Aaron Copland, two sets, Boosey and Hawkes.

Old English Melodies. Wilson, ed., Boosey and Hawkes. $16.00.

One Hundred English Folksongs. Cecil Sharp, ed., medium, Dover Publishing. $11.95.

Pathways of Song. Frank Laforge and Will Earhart, eds., four volumes, each is available in high and low, Warner Bros. Pub. $8.95.

Popular Ballads for Classical Singers. Richard Walters, ed., high and low, with and without cassette, G. Schirmer. $16.95.

Reliquary of English Song. Frank Hunter Potter, ed., volume one, G. Shirmer. $11.95.

Romantic American Art Songs. Richard Walters, ed., high, G. Schirmer. $16.95.

Samuel Barber Collected Songs. high and low, G. Schirmer. $19.95.

The Second Book of [Soprano, Mezzo-Soprano, Tenor, Baritone/Bass] Solos. compiled by Joan Boytim, with or without CD, Hal Leonard. $10.95.

Seven Elizabethan Lyrics. Roger Quilter, high, low, Boosey and Hawkes. $6.95.

The Singing Road. Ward, ed., three volumes in high, med, and low, Carl Fischer. $10.50.

Songs for Low Voice in a Comfortable Range. with and without cassette, Carl Fischer. $12.95-19.95.

Song through the Centuries: 41 Vocal Reptertoire Pieces from the 17th through the 20th Centuries. Bernard Taylor, ed., high, low, Carl Fischer. $12.95.

The Songs of John Jacob Niles. medium high and medium low, G. Schirmer.

Standard Vocal Repertoire. Richard D. Row, ed., two volumes, high and low, R.D. Row Music Co. $9.95.

Thirty Spirituals. Hall Johnson, ed., G. Schirmer. $15.95.

Three Shakespeare Songs. Roger Quilter, first set, high, low, Boosey and Hawkes. $10.00.

Twelve Songs. Mozart, John Glenn Paton, ed., high, medium, Alfred Publishing Co. $8.95.

Twenty-Four Italian Songs and Arias of the Seventeenth and Eighteenth Centuries. medium high, medium low, with or without cassette, G. Schirmer. $5.95-10.95.

Twenty-Six Italian Songs. John Glenn Paton, ed., medium high and medium low, with and without cassette, Alfred Publishing. $7.95-18.90.

The Young Singer. Richard D. Row, ed., soprano, contralto/mezzo, tenor, bar/bass, R. D. Row Music. $9.95.

Broadway Anthologies

The First Book of Broadway Solos. compiled by Joan Boytim, soprano, mezzo-soprano, tenor, baritone/bass, Hal Leonard. $10.95.

Sacred Anthologies

Hymn Classics. Richard Walter, high and low, with or without CD, Hal Leonard. $17.95.

Sacred Songs for All Occasions. high and low, R.D. Row Music. $8.50.

Songs of Praise by Contemporary Composers. Darwin Wolford, ed., Harold Flammer, Inc.

The Song Book. (contemporary Christian), two volumes, Myrrh Music. $16.95.

Vendors

It's a good idea to patronize your local music store. They are friends of the arts, and you should be their friend by patronizing them when you can. However, if your store is unwilling or unable to get music for you in a reasonable time, consider mail order. Almost all mail order music vendors service phone orders rapidly when you pay with a credit card. Most music orders are delayed because (1) they waited for your check to clear; (2) you did not specify the mode of shipment; (3) you ordered an item they did not have in stock; or (4) the item was temporarily out of print. It is usually better to find a vendor who has the item you want in stock than to wait indefinitely for your favorite vendor to order it.

Menchey Music Service, Inc.
80 Wetzel Dr.
Hanover, PA 17042
717-637-2185
800-872-2917

Stanton's Sheet Music
Import Division
330 S. 4th St.
Columbus, OH 43215
614-224-4257

J. Patelson Music House
160 W. 56th St.
New York, NY 10019
212-582-5840
800-733-1474

T.I.S. Music Shop
1302 E. 3rd St.
PO Box 669
Bloomington, IN 47402
800-421-8132

Music Theatre Resources

Monologues

Monologue books are an important resource for singers auditioning for straight plays or musicals that require a monologue as part of the audition. They are also a good resource for singers who are increasing their communication skills by taking an acting class. Two publishers, Dramaline, and Smith and Kraus, publish series of monologue and scene books. The books listed here cover a wide variety of materials including monologues from great literature.

Bolton, Barbara, and John Richmond, eds. *New Drama-Men: A Selection of Fifty Speeches for Actors.* New York: Samuel French, 1966.

Craig, David. *A Performer Prepares: A Guide to Song Preparation for Actors, Singers and Dancers.* New York: Applause Theatre Books, 1993.

Earley, Michael, and Philippa Keil, eds. *Solo: The Best Monologues of the 80's (Men).* New York: Applause Theatre Books, 1987.

——. *Solo: The Best Monologues of the 80's (Women).* New York: Applause Theatre Books, 1987.

——. *The Contemporary Monologue (Men).* New York: Routledge, 1995.

——. *The Contemporary Monologue (Women).* New York: Routledge, 1996.

Emerson, Robert, and Jane Grunbach, eds. *Monologues: Men: 50 Speeches from Contemporary Theater.* New York: Drama Book Publishers, Vol. 1, 1976, Vol. 2, 1983, Vol. 3, 1989.

——. *Monologues: Women: 50 Speeches from Contemporary Theater.* New York: Drama Book Publishers, Vol. 1, 1976, Vol. 2, 1982, Vol. 3, 1989.

Harrington, Laura, ed. *100 Monologues: An Audition Sourcebook from New Dramatists.* New York: Mentor, 1989.

Karsher, Roger, ed. *Neil Simon Monologues.* Rancho Mirage, CA: Dramaline, 1996.

Morris, Karen, ed. *The Monologue Index.* Lyme, NH: Smith and Kraus, 1995.

Pike, Frank, and Thomas G. Dunn. *Scenes and Monologues for the New American Theater.* New York: New American Library, 1988.

Poggi, Jack. *The Monologue Workshop.* New York: Applause Theatre

Books, 1990.

Rudnicki, Stefan, ed. *The Actor's Book of Monologues for Women from Non-Dramatic Sources.* New York: Penguin Books, 1991.

——. *The Actor's Book of Classical Monologues.* New York: Penguin, 1988.

Schulman, Michael, and Eva Meklar, eds. *The Actor's Scenebook: Scenes and Monologues from Contemporary Plays.* New York: Bantam Books, Vol. 1, 1984. Vol. 2, 1987.

Seto, Judith Robert. *The Young Actor's Workbook: A Collection of Specially Chosen Scenes and Monologues with Directions for the Actor.* New York: Grove Press, 1979.

Shengold, Nina. *The Actor's Book of Contemporary Stage Monologues.* New York: Penguin, 1987.

Smith, Marisa, and Kristin Graham, eds. *Monologues from Literature.* New York: Fawcett Columbine, 1992

Temchin, Jack, ed. *One on One: Best Monologues for the Nineties.* New York: Applause Theatre Books, 1996.

Songs

An excellent list of songs graded by voice type, difficulty, and tempo is found in "Teaching Musical Theatre Songs: A Graded Repertoire List" by David Alt and Novie Green in *The Journal of Singing* (Jan/Feb 1996, p 25-32). Songs from this list are readily available from Hal Leonard Publishers, who seem to have a lock on most of the Broadway repertoire. Another very interesting list of songs is found in the final chapter of Fred Silver's *Auditioning for the Musical Theatre* (New York: Penguin, 1985, p 184-201). These songs are less readily available, but have interesting observations about them to motivate your search. Thirteen songs are listed in David Craig's *A Performer Prepares* (New York: Applause Theatre Books, 1993). This book has complete explanations of interpretation via dialogues with the student. Following is a list of songs chosen from five very accessible sources. They are listed in voice categories with the easiest songs first. The categories conform to those commonly used in casting. However, if you see a song you like in another category and it fits your voice, your communication skills, your type, and the rules of the audition—go for it!

Sources

1. *The Singer's Musical Theatre Anthology,* edited by Richard Walters. (New York: Hal Leonard, 1986) Soprano

2. *The Singer's Musical Theatre Anthology,* edited by Richard Walters. (New York: Hal Leonard, 1986) Mezzo/Alto
3. *The Singer's Musical Theatre Anthology,* edited by Richard Walters. (New York: Hal Leonard, 1986) Tenor
4. *The Singer's Musical Theatre Anthology,* edited by Richard Walters. (New York: Hal Leonard, 1986) Baritone/Bass
5. *The Definitive Broadway Collection* (New York: Hal Leonard, 1988)

Women's High Voice Ballads

Song	*Source*
Where or when	1
Bewitched	2,5
Far from the home I love	1
Till there was you	1
Can't help lovin'dat man of mine	1
My ship	1
So in love	1
Goodnight my someone	5
Falling in love with love	1
If I loved you	1
Somebody, somewhere	1
Not a day goes by	1
What good will the moon be	1
He touched me	5
One more kiss	1
Come rain or come shine	5
Green finch and linnet bird	1

Women's High Voice Up-tempo

If I were a bell	5
I enjoy being a girl	5
Mr. Snow	1
Comedy tonight (à la Whoopi Goldberg)	5
Button up your overcoat	5
That'll show him	1
My heart belongs to daddy	5
Many a new day	1
Much more	1

I got rhythm   5

Women's Medium/Low Voice Ballad

As long as he needs me   5
The party's over   5
Anyone can whistle   2
My funny valentine   2
The miller's son   2
He wasn't you   2
If he walked into my life   5
Don't cry for me Argentina   2
What I did for love   5
I don't know how to love him   5

Women's Medium/Low Voice Up-tempo

I cain't say no   2
There's a small hotel   5
Always true to you in my fashion   2
I ain't down yet   5
Could I leave you   2
Saga of Jenny   2
We need a little Christmas   5

Men's High Voice Ballad

Old devil moon   5
Wish you were here   3
I could write a book   5
Being alive   3
Maria   5
Many moons ago   3
Lonely house   3
Love, I hear   3
Fanny   3

Men's High Voice Up-tempo

This can't be love   5
When I'm not with the girl I love   3

If you could see her	3
On the street where you live	3
Kansas city	3
You've got to be carefully taught	3
She loves me	5

Men's Medium/Low Voice Ballad

It's all right with me	5
Try to remember	5
Johanna	4
Soliloquy	4
Lost in the stars	4
If ever I would leave you	4
Lonely room	4
Meditation I	4

Men's Medium/Low Voice Up-tempo

Mame	5
This can't be love	4
Once in love with Amy	5
C'est moi	4
How to handle a woman	4
Mack the knife	4,5
Everybody says don't	4
I am I, Don Quixote	4
They call the wind Maria	4
A red-headed woman	4
Where is the life that late I led	4
If this isn't love	5

Sample Worksheet for *A Beginning Singer's Guide*

Pages 1-46

1. Why do you want to sing?

2. In what musical style do you prefer to sing, and why should you study other styles?

3. Outline the vocal mechanism.

4. Pretend you are the teacher showing a new student how to breathe. Write out your instructions.

5. The glottal stroke will cause the vocal folds to _____

6. The appoggio is _____

7. We hear ourselves differently than others do because _____
   _____

8. Gola aperta is _____

9. Name four methods for promoting gola aperta_____
   _____
   _____

10. The five cartilages of the larynx are _____
   _____
   _____

11. The larger the cavity, the _____the frequency to which it re-sponds.

12. Vibrato is _____
   _____

13. Write about an instance in a piece you are singing that requires you to modify a vowel sound.

Song/Aria Study Guide

Student name:_____

Today's date:_____ Due date:_____

Title:_____

Composer:_____

Composer's dates and date of composition:_____

Short biography of composer and events surrounding composition :

_____

_____

_____

_____

Part of a cycle or a set? Summarize:_____

_____

Ref cited:_____

Poet:_____

Poet's dates and date of poem:_____

Short biography of poet and events surrounding poem:_____

_____

_____

_____

Part of a cycle or set? Summarize:_____

_____

Reference cited:_____

Musical analysis overview

Melody:_____

_____

Harmony:_____

_____

Texture:_____

_____

Tempo:_____

Text setting:_____

_____

Technical problems with:_____

_____

_____

_____

_____

Song/Aria Study Guide (cont.)

Answer the following interpretive questions (the five Ws).

What is the mood of the song and how is it related in text and music?

_____

_____

_____

Who is the speaker?_____

Who or what does he or she speak to?_____

What is the speaker's subtext?_____

What is the listener's subtext?_____

What does the speaker perceive through all five senses?_____

_____

What is the speaker's physical and emotional state?_____

What is the listener's physical and emotional state?_____

What is the speaker's history?_____

What is the speaker's history with the listener?_____

What is the standing of their relationship?_____

What happens when the text ends?_____

What happens when the music ends?_____

Where is the speaker?_____

Where is the listener?_____

When does the action of the song occur, and what effect

does it have on the speaker and listener?_____

Why am I singing instead of speaking? (What is my intention?)___

_____

Why is the listener listening? (What is his or her intention?)_____

_____

Why does my emotional state change?_____

_____

Why does the listener's emotional state change?_____

_____

Why does the listener respond?_____

On a copy of the song include a word-for-word translation of the song
and a third line analysis of the music.

Voice Student Questionnaire

Name_____

Age_____ Phone Number_____

How long have you studied voice ?_____

Where and with whom have you studied voice?_____
_____.

Have you ever been to _____operas _____musicals_____classical
concerts with singers?

Have you ever been in _____operas _____musicals_____classical
concerts with singers? If so, list a few of each._____
_____
_____

What singers do you listen to? _____

Who is your idol among singers?_____

What was the last CD you bought?_____

Tell me about the last time you felt emotional involved with your
singing._____
_____

Are you allergic to anything?_____

Do you have any chronic health problems?_____

Do you take any medication?_____

Do you think you have any health problems that affect your singing?
_____

Have you ever been hoarse for more than a week_____, or been
a cheerleader___?

Who encouraged you to sing?_____
_____

What do your parents think about your singing?_____

Why do you want to study singing?_____
_____

Teacher Comments After Audition

Range   Respiration   Phonation
_____
_____

Resonation   Articulation   Motivation
_____

Predicted voice type_____

Practice Details

Time In and Out	Goals and Materials	Study Method	Accomp? √

Sample Jury Sheet

Student name_____ Date_____
Jury repertoire_____

RESPIRATION
    Breath inadequate at_____
    Method suspect at_____
    Method audible or visible at_____
*Comments*_____

PHONATION
    Larynx not at rest at _____
    Poor onset and offset at_____
    Unnecessary glottal at_____
*Comments*_____

RESONATION
    Poor timbre choices at _____
    Too dark at _____
    Too bright at_____
*Comments*_____

ARTICULATION
    Diction unclear at _____
    Check these vowels_____

*Comments*_____

INTERPRETATION
    Mood_____
    Tempo_____
    Phrasing_____
    Dynamics_____
*Comments*_____

PRESENTATION
Comments on the back include ensemble, acting choices, style, concentration, facial expression, and stage appearance.

Vocalises

The vocalises on the next pages are a reference for voice teachers and future voice teachers. They are not for indiscriminate use by the young singer. Singing vocalises incorrectly or selecting vocalises that build the wrong muscle groups for a particular stage of development will do the young singer more harm than good. The vocalises presented are divided into the categories of technique building. No matter how carefully constructed, a vocalise can't work on a single facet of vocal technique without affecting the others. The voice is an integrated instrument and requires an integrated approach to its development. For this reason, it is better to use some examples from each technical area to build the voice, than to decide that a student's problem is head voice and do nothing but head voice vocalises.

The vocalises should look familiar to you, as they have been in the common vocabulary of voice teachers for a long time; so long, in fact, that nobody can say with assurance where they came from or how they may have changed over time. I have shorthanded many of the exercises to save space and include some directions here if you are unfamiliar with the exercise. Most of the text in the exercises is IPA as it can be expressed on a the standard keyboard of a music writing program. Hence E is [ɛ], O is [ɔ], I is [ɪ], U is [ʊ], and A is [ɑ].

Breath Exercises (numbers refer to the exercise number)
1. Exercise to be repeated in shorter note values of eighths, sixteenths, as duplets and triplets.
3. Aspirate *h* is added to the vowel. All the vowels are eventually sung.
4. Begin a long tone with aspirate *h* plus any vowel and add abdominal support to propel the *k*. Young singers who have no sensation of abdominal support are good candidates for this exercise.
6. A corollary exercise to 4. Instead of engaging abdominal support at the end of the word, propel the *f* with it at the beginning.

Head Voice/Range
1. The NG as in si*ng*.
6. JU is [jʊ].
8. First text is German (kind of!).
10. Cascade is siren descending and can be the full range of the voice.

Agility

9. The pulsated drill is an airflow articulation, not a laryngeal one. It is created by pulses of air. It begins as a fairly large movement observed as the upward motion of the epigastrium. As it progresses in speed it becomes so small and fast as to be unobservable. A run is eventually substituted for the one-note drill. The resulting run should be clean and without *h*'s or the hint of staccato.

Register Blending

13. Arpeggi high to low with close-open-close succession of vowels and open-close-open succession of vowels.

14. Try creating all the timbres in the middle voice. Practice messa di voce on all the vowels and in all ranges.

BREATH EXERCISES

1.

HA (repeat)

Ho (in eighths, triplets, and sixteenths)

2.

Any Vowel   Observe Breaths

3.

H plus any Vowel

4.

[H u k] soft - engage abdominal support

5.

[S]   and exhale

6.

Engage abdominal support for the 'F' in fist

HEAD VOICE/RANGE

AGILITY

REGISTER BLENDING

7.

M————— A————— M—————
(reverse)

A————— M————— A—————

8.

NA————— O————— A

9.

BEL LA SI- GNO————— RA————

10.

i——— e——— a——— o——— u

11.

i——— o——— a————— i———

12.

YA   YA   YA   YA   YU   YU

13.

Arps:
High to Low and back,
C - O - C Vowels and
reverse

14.

Voice Timbre Terms:
voce___ bianca, aperta, chuisa,
coperta, petto, testa, cupo, finta,
agguistamento. Messa di voce $<>$

SOFT PALATE

KI KE KI KE KI

KA KE KI KOKU (ETC)

KI KA KI KA KI

ki ki (etc)

FOCUS/LINE/
ARTICULATION

1. IMPOSTO

M-   A- (E or i)

2. LINE

Si   I   e   E   a   o   O   U   u
see sid say said saw sod sew soot sue

3.

Si   SO   Si

4.

Mi ME MA MO MU--

also V, TH and F

5.

N--   (all vowels)

6.

(all Cons. and Vowels)

7.

La Le Li Lo   (etc)

References

Abo-El-Enene, N. (1967). Functional anatomy of the larynx. Thesis. University of London.

Acker, B. F. (1987). Vocal tract adjustments for the projected voice. *Journal of Voice* 1, (1), 77-82.

Allanbrook, W. J. (1983). *Rhythmic gesture in Mozart.* Chicago: University of Chicago Press. 174-177.

Atkinson, R. C. & Shiffrin, R. M. (1968). Human memory: A proposed system and its control processes. In K. Spence and J. Spence (Eds.), *The Psychology of Learning and Motivation,* (Vol. 2). New York: Academic Press.

Atkinson, R. L., Atkinson, R. C., Smith, E. E. & Bem, D. J. (1993). *Introduction to psychology,* (11th ed.). New York: Harcourt, Brace and Jovanovich, 671-693.

Baken, R. J. (1987). Clinical measurement of speech and voice. New York: College Hill.

Balk, W. (1985). *The complete singer-actor,* (2nd ed.). Minneapolis: University of Minnesota Press, 95.

_____. (1991) *The radiant performer.* Minneapolis: University of Minnesota Press, 214-339.

Barham T. J. & Nelson D. L. (1991). *The boy's changing voice.* Miami, FL: Belwin Mills.

Bloom B. S. (1956). *Taxonomy of educational objectives. Handbook I:*

Cognitive domain. New York: David McKay.

———. (1964)*Taxonomy of educational objectives. Handbook II: Affective domain.* New York: David McKay.

Brodnitz F. S. (1983). Treatment of post mutational voice disorders, in W. H. Perkins, (ed.), *Voice disorders.* New York: Thieme-Stratton, 69-73.

Brown, W. E. (1931). *Vocal wisdom: maxims of Giovanni Battista Lamperti.* Boston: Crescendo Press, Reprint.

Caldwell, R. (1990).*The performer prepares.* Dallas: Pst...Inc., 84-104.

Corn, E. & Haupt-Nolen, P. (1985). Career guide for young American singers. 25:4, iv.

Cleveland, T. F. (1994). A clearer view of singing voice production: 25 years of progress, *Journal of Voice* 8:1, 18-23.

———. (1997). Voice pedagogy degree programs: Part IV, *Journal of Singing 53:5,* 51.

Collins, D. (1993). *Teaching choral music.* Englewood Cliffs, NJ: Prentice- Hall.

Cooke, J. F. (1948). *How to memorize music.* Philadelphia:Theodore Presser Co.

Cooksey, J. M. (1992). *Working with the adolescent voice.* St. Louis: Concordia Pub.

Dorneman, Joan. (1992) *Complete preparation.* New York: Excalibur.

Easty, D. E. (1981). *On method acting.* New York: Ivy Books.

Eich, J. E. (1980). The cue dependent nature of state dependent retrieval. *Memory and Cognition,* 8, 157-173.

Ehret, W. (1959). *The conductor's handbook.* Milwaukee, WI: Hal Leonard.

Ely, M. C. (1991). Stop performance anxiety! *Music Educator's Journal* 79, 35-39.

Elliot, N., Sundberg, J. & Gramming, P. (1995) What happens during vocal warm-up? *Journal of Voice,* 9, 37-44.

Emmons, S. & Sonntag, S (1979). *The Art of the Song Recital.* New York: Norton.

Garcia, M. (the son). (undated) *Garcia's complete school of singing.* London: Creamer, Beale and Chappell. This is a compilation of editions from 1847 and 1872.

———.(1840). *Memoire sur la voix humaine presentè a l'academie des sciences in 1840.* Paris: E. Suverger.

———.(1894). *Hints on singing.* Translated by Beata Garcia. London: Ascherberg, Hopwood and Crew .

Gagne, R. M. (1985). *The conditions of learning and theory of instruction (4th ed.).* New York:Holt, Rhinehart and Winston.

Gardner, H. (1983). *Frames of mind: The theory of multiple intelligences.* New York: Basic Books

_____. (1993). *Multiple intelligences: The theory in practice.* New York: Basic Books.

Gardner H. & Hatch T. (1989). Multiple intelligences go to school: Educational implications of the theory of multiple intelligences. *Educational Researcher,* 18: 4-10.

Gates, G. A. (1988). Performance anxiety (stage fright): Causes and control. *NATS Journal,* Nov./Dec., 26-27.

Gould, W. J. & Korovin, G.S. (1994). Laboratory Advances for Voice Measurements. *Journal of Voice,* 8:1, 8-17.

Griffin, B., Woo, P., Colton, R., Casper, J. & Brewer, D. (1995). Physiological characteristics of the supported singing voice. A preliminary study. *Journal of Voice,* 9:1, 45-56.

Grubb, T. (1979). *Singing in French: A manual of French diction and French vocal repertoire.* New York: Schirmer Books.

Hamann, D. L. (1985). The other side of stage fright. *Music Educators Journal,* 71 (Apr), 26-28.

Harris, S. R. (1986). A psychologist views musical performance anxiety. *American Music Teacher,* 35, 24-5+.

Helfgot, D. & Beeman, W. (1993). *The third line.* New York: Schirmer Books.

Hirano, M., Kurita, S. & Kakashima, T. (1981). The structure of the vocal folds. In K. N. Stevens, & M. Hirans, (Eds). *Vocal fold physiology.* Tokyo: University of Tokyo Press, 33-45.

Hirano, M. & Sato, K. (1993). *Histological color atlas of the human larynx.* San Diego, CA: Singular Publishing.

Hixon, T. J. (1983). Voice disorders in relation to respiratory kinematics. *Seminars in Speech and Language,* 4: 217-31.

Intons-Petersen, M. J. & Smith, M. M. (1987). The anatomy of repertory memory. *Learning, Memory and Cognition,* 13, 490-500.

Isshiki, N. (1965). Vocal intensity and airflow rate. *Folia Phoniatrica* 17:92-104.

Kahan, S. (1985). *Introduction to acting,* (2nd Edition). Newton, MA: Allyn and Bacon.

Krechevsky, M. (1991). Project spectrum: An innovative assessment alternative. *Educational Leadership,* 48:43-48.

Kuiken, D. (Ed.) (1991). *Mood and memory.* Newbury Park, CA: Sage

Publications.

Lamperti, F. (undated). *The Art of Singing,* translated by J.C. Griffith, New York: G. Schirmer.

Lehrer, P. M. (1987). A review of the approaches to the management of tension and stage fright in music performance. *Journal of Research in Music Education,* 35 (3), 143-152.

Levarie S. (1952). *Le Nozze di Figaro.* Chicago: University of Chicago Press. 209-218.

Mager, J. (1992). *Preparing Educational Objectives,* (2nd Ed). Palo Alto, CA: Fearon.

Mann W. (1977). *The operas of Mozart.* New York: Oxford University Press. 430-433.

Marchesi, M. (1901). *Ten singing lessons.* New York: Harper and Brothers.

Matthay, T. (1926). *Memorizing and playing from memory.* London: Oxford University Press.

McCune, B. A. (1982). *Functional performance anxiety modification in adult pianists.* Diss. Teachers College, Columbia University. University Microfilms #8501103.

McKenzie, D. (1956). *Training the boy's changing voice.* New Brunswick, NJ: Rutgers University Press.

Miller, R. (1986). The structure of singing: System and art in vocal technique. New York: G. Schirmer.

_____.(1993). *Training tenor voices.* New York: Schirmer Books.

Moberly, R. (1968). *Three Mozart operas.* New York: Dodd, Mead & Co. 132-135.

Nagel, J., Himle, D. & Papsdorf, J. (1981). Coping with performance anxiety. *NATS Bulletin,* Mar/Apr, 26-33.

Neiser, U. (1976). *Cognition and reality.* New York: Appleton, Century, Crofts Inc.

Noice, Helga (1992). Elaborative memory strategies of professional actors. *Applied Cognitive Psychology,* 6, 417-427.

Nuki, M. (1984). Memorization of piano music. *Psychologia,* 27,157-163.

Owens, R. (1984). *The professional singer's guide to New York.* Dallas, TX: American Institute of Musical Studies.

Pagano, C., Valentino, T. & Baddeley, A. (1991). Short term memory and foreign language vocabulary learning. *Journal of Memory and Language,* 30, 331-369.

Pressley, M., Levin, J. R. & Delaney, H. D. (1982). The mnemonic keyword method. *Review of Educational Research, 52,* 61-91.

Raphael, B. N. & Scherer, R. C. (1987). Voice modifications of stage actors: Acoustic analyses. *Journal of Voice* 1: 1, 83-87.

Reubart, D. (1985). *Anxiety and musical performance.* New York: Da Capo Press, 181-208.

Reyman, R. G. (1983). Stage fright? never! mental attitudes for a successful performance. *The Instrumentalist,* 38, Dec., 15-17.

Roe, P. F. (1994) *Choral music,* (2nd Ed.). Prospect Heights, IL: Waveland Press.

Ross, E. (1964). Improving facility in music memorization. *Journal of Research in Music Education,* 12, 269-278.

Robinson, R. & Winold, A. (1992). *The Choral Experience.* Prospect Heights, IL: Waveland Press.

Sabol, J. W, Lee, L., & Stemple J.C. (1995). The value of vocal exercises in the practice regimen of singers. *Journal of Voice,* 9:1, 27-36.,

Serafine, M. L., Crowder, R. G. & Repp, B. (1984). Integration of melody and text in memory for song. *Journal of Memory and Language,* 25, 123-135.

Seashore, C. E. (1936). Psychology of the vibrato in voice and instrument. *University of Iowa Studies in the Psychology of Music,* 3:7.

Shurtleff, M. (1978). *Audition.* New York: Bantam Books.

Silver, F. (1985). *Auditioning for the musical theater.* New York. Newmarket Press.

Spolin, V. (1985). *Theater games for rehearsal.* Evanston, IL: Northwestern University Press

_____.*Theater games for the classroom.* Evanston,IL: Northwestern Univer. Press.

Smith, S. M., Glenberg, A., & Bjork, R.A. (1978). Environmental context and human memory. *Memory and Cognition,* 6, 342-353.

Stanislavski, C. (1936). *An actor prepares.* New York: Theatre Art Books, 158.

_____. (1948) *My life and art.* New York: Theater Art Books.

Stemple, J. C., Lee, L., D'Amico, B., & Pickup, B. (1994). Efficacy of vocal function exercises as a method of improving voice production. *Journal of Voice,* 8:3, 271-278.

Strasberg, L. (1987). *A dream of passion.* New York: Plume Books.

Swanson, F. J. (1973). *Music teaching in the junior high and middle school.* Englewood Cliffs, NJ: Prentice-Hall

Titze, I. (1994). *Principles of voice production.* Englewood Cliffs, NJ; Prentice Hall.

Tosi, P. F. (1743) *Observations on the florid song,* translated by J.E. Galliard. London: J. Wilcox.

Williams, B. B., Larson, G. W., & Price, D. W. (1964). An investigation of selected female singing-and-speaking-voice characteristics through comparison of a group of pre-menarcheal girls to a group of post-menarcheal girls. *Journal of Singing,* 53, no. 3 (Jan/Feb 1996): 33-39+.

Williamson, S.C. (1964). The effect of special instruction of speed, transfer, and retention in memorizing songs. Diss. Univ. of Kansas.

Wilson, J. P. (1983). The effect of sleep and time on music memory. Diss. California State at Stanislaus.

Selected Bibliography

The following bibliography represents some of the books and articles that the author has found to be of worth in his personal reading over the years, and hence contributed to this book. The student should use it as a guide to further reading in subjects he or she finds of interest. Many of the texts are available in school libraries. Some others may require the use of interlibrary loan.

Acting
Adler, Stella. *The Technique of Acting*. New York: Bantam Books, 1988.

Balk, Wesley. *The Complete Singer-Actor*. Minneapolis: University of Minnesota Press, 1973.

_____. *Performing Power*. Minneapolis: University of Minnesota Press, 1985.

_____. *The Radiant Performer*. Minneapolis: University of Minnesota Press, 1991.

Bernardi, Philip. *Improvisation Starters*. Cincinnati, OH: Betterway Books, 1992.

Caldwell, Robert. *The Performer Prepares*. Dallas: Pst . . . Inc, 1990.

Cohen, Robert. *Acting Power*. Palo Alto, CA: Mayfield Publishing, 1978.

Delgado, Ramon. *Acting with Both Sides of Your Brain*. New York: Holt, Rinehart and Winston, 1986.

Easty, Dwight Edward. *On Method Acting*. New York. Ivy Books, 1981.

Felsenstein, Walter. *The Music Theater of Walter Felsenstein*. New York: Norton, 1975.

Glenn, Stanley L. *The Complete Actor*. Boston: Allyn and Bacon, 1977.

Green, Barry. *The Inner Game of Music*. New York: Doubleday, 1986.

Hodgson, John, and Ernest Richards. *Improvisation*. New York: Grove Press, 1966.

Kahan, Stanley. *Introduction to Acting*. (2nd Ed.). Newton, MA: Allyn and Bacon, 1985.

McGaw, Charles. *Acting Is Believing*. New York: Holt, Rinehart and Winston, 1980.

Meisner, Sanford, and Dennis Longwell. *On Acting*. New York: Vintage Books, 1987.

Miller, Allan. *A Passion for Acting*. New York: Backstage Books, 1992.

Novak, Elaine Adams. *Performing in Musicals*. New York: Schirmer Books, 1988.

Shurtleff, Michael. *Audition*. New York: Bantam Books, 1978.

Silver, Fred. *Auditioning for the Musical Theater*. New York: Newmarket Press, 1985.

Spolin, Viola. *Theater Games for the Classroom*. Evanston, IL: Northwestern University. Press, 1986.

———. *Theater Games for Rehearsal*. Evanston, IL: Northwestern University Press, 1985.

Stanislavski, Constantin. *My Life and Art*. New York: Theatre Art Books, 1948.

———. *An Actor Prepares*. New York: Theatre Art Books, 1936.

Stanislavski, Constantin, and Pavel Rumyantsev. *Stanislavski on Opera*. NewYork: Theatre Arts Books, 1975.

———. *Creating a Role*. New York: Theatre Arts Book, 1961.

———. *Building a Character*. New York: Theatre Arts Books,1949.

———. *Stanislavski on Opera*. New York: Theatre Arts Books, 1975.

———. *An Actor's Handbook*. New York: Theatre Arts Books, 1963.

Strasberg, Lee. *A Dream of Passion*. New York: Plume Books, 1987.

Vineberg, Steve. *Method Actors: Three Generations of an American Acting Style*. New York: Schirmer Books, 1991.

Wilson, G. D. (1991). *Psychology and the Performing Arts*. Amsterdam: Swets and Zeitlinger

Choral Conducting

Barham, Terry J., and Darolyne L. Nelson. *The Boy's Changing Voice*. Miami, FL: Belwin Mills, 1991.

Boyd, Jack. *The Rehearsal Guide for the Choral Conductor*. Champaign, IL: Mark Foster, 1970.

Ehret, Walter. *The Choral Conductor's Handbook*. Milwaukee: Hal Leonard, 1959.

Cooksey, John M. *Working with the Adolescent Voice*. St. Louis: Concordia Publishing House, 1992.

Gordon, Lewis. *The Director's Complete Handbook*. West Nyack, NY: Parker, 1977.

Robinson, Ray, and Allen Winold. *The Choral Experience*. Prospect Heights, IL: Waveland Press, 1992.

Diction

Colorni, Evalina. *Singer's Italian*. New York: Schirmer Books, 1970.

De Boor, Helmut, Moser, Hugo and Christian Winkler. *Siebs Deutsche Aussprache: Reine und gemaessigte Hochlautung mit Aussprachewoerterbuch*. 19th rev. ed. Berlin: De Gruyter, 1984.

Grubb, Thomas. *Singing in French: A Manual of French Diction & French Vocal Repertoire*. New York: Schirmer Books, 1979.

Marshall, Madeleine. *The Singer's Manual of English Diction*. New York: Schirmer Books, 1953.

Moriarty, John. *Diction*. Boston: E. C. Schirmer Books, 1975.

Odom, William. *German for Singers: A Textbook of Diction & Phonetics*. New York: Shirmer Books, 1981.

Moriarty, John. *Diction*. Boston: E. C. Schirmer, 1975.

Uris, Dorothy. *To Sing in English*. New York: Boosey and Hawkes, 1971.

Wall, Joan. *The International Phonetic Alphabet for Singers*. Dallas: Pst . . . Inc., 1990.

_____.*Diction for Singers*. Dallas: Pst . . . Inc., 1991.

Dictionaries

The foreign language dictionaries published by Bantam Books usually are sufficient for undergraduates. They combine a very modest price with entries written in IPA. The following are often consulted as well.

Betteridge, Harold T. *The New Cassell's German Dictionary.* New York: Funk and Wagnalls, 1965.

Casselli, Lucia Incerti. *Il Nuovo Dizionario Inglese Garzanti.* Milano: Redazioni Garzanti, 1984.

DuBois, Marguerite-Marie. *Modern French-English Dictionary.* Paris: Librairie Larousse, 1960.

Kenyon, J. S. Thomas Knott. *A Pronouncing Dictionary of American English.* Springfield, MA: G. & C. Merriam,1944.

Electronics

Baragary, Ray. *The Billboard Guide to Home Recording.* New York: Billboard Books, 1996.

Bartlett, Bruce, and Jenny Bartlett. "Tricks of the Trade." *Stereo Review.* (Dec. 1994): 101-104.

Eargle, John. "The First Step to Great Sound." *Stereo Review.* (Dec. 1993): 99-102.

Elliott, Robert. "Improving Ensemble Recordings." *The Instrumentalist.* (May 1994): 56.

Ephland, John. "A Crafty Art." *Downbeat.* (May 1994): 6.

Frost, Thomas. "Recordings—The Editing Process." *The Piano Quarterly* 151: 28-32.

Hurtig, Brent. "Making Tracks." *Keyboard Magazine.* (Mar. 1993): 115.

_____. (May 1993): 123.

_____. (June 1993): 109+.

_____. (July 1993): 117.

McIan, Peter, and Larry Wickman. *The Musician's Guide to Home Recording.* New York: Amsco, 1994.

Molenda, Michael. "In Your Face." *Electronic Musician.* (May 1994): 44-53.

Rapaport, Diane. *How to Make and Sell Your Own Recording.* 4th ed. Englewood Cliffs, NJ: Prentice-Hall, 1992.

Yeo, Douglas. "Winning an Orchestral Audition." *International Musician* (Nov. 1992): 4-5.

General Pedagogy

Alderson, Richard. *The Complete Handbook of Voice Training.* West Nyack, NY: Parker Publishing, 1979.

Appelman, D. Ralph. *The Science of Vocal Pedagogy.* Bloomington, IN: Indiana University Press, 1967.

Brodnitz, Friedrich S. *Keep Your Voice Healthy*. New York: Harper and Brothers, 1953.

Brown, William Earl. *Vocal Wisdom: Maxims of Giovanni Battista Lamperti*. Boston: Crescendo Press, 1973.

Burgin, John Carroll. *Teaching Singing*. Metuchen, NJ: Scarecrow Press, 1973.

Coffin, Berton. *Overtones of Bel Canto*. Metuchen, NJ: Scarecrow Press, 1980.

David, Marilee. *The New Voice Pedagogy*. Lanham, MD: Scarecrow Press, 1995.

Dowling, W. Jay, and Dane L. Harwood. *Music Cognition*. Orlando, FL: Academic Press, 1986.

Duey, Philip. *Bel Canto in Its Golden Age*. New York: King's Crown Press, 1950.

Fields, Victor Alexander. *Training the Singing Voice*. New York: King's Crown Press, 1947.

Garcia, Manuel. *Garcia's Complete School of Singing*. London: Cramer, Beale and Chappell.

_____. *Memoire sur la voix humaine*. Paris: E. Surverger, 1849.

_____. *Hints on Singing*. New York: Schuberth & Co., 1894.

Heaton, Wallace, and C. W. Hargens. eds. *An Interdisciplinary Index of Studies in Physics, Medicine and Music Related to the Human Voice*.Bryn Mawr:Theodore Presser, 1968.

Helfgot, Daniel and William Beeman. *The Third Line*. New York: Schirmer Books, 1993.

Hines, Jerome. *Great Singers on Great Singing*. New York: Doubleday, 1982.

Lamperti, Francesco. *The Art of Singing*. New York: G. Schirmer, (n.d.)

McKinney, James.*The Diagnosis and Correction of Vocal Faults*. Nashville: Broadman Press, 1982.

Miller, Richard. *English, French, German and Italian Techniques of Singing*. Metuchen, NJ: Scarecrow Press, 1977.

_____. *The Structure of Singing*. New York: Schirmer Books, 1986.

_____. *Training Tenor Voices*. New York: Schirmer Books, 1993.

Owens, Richard. *The Professional Singer's Guide to New York*. Dallas: American Institute of Musical Studies, 1984.

Reubart, Dale. *Anxiety and Musical Performance*. New York: Da Capo Press, 1985.

Rich, Maria, ed. *Career Guide for the Young American Singer*. New

York: Central Opera Service, 1986
Sundberg, Johan. *The Science of the Singing Voice*. Dekalb, IL.: Northern Illinois Press, 1987.
Titze, Ingo R. *Principles of Voice Production*. Englewood Cliffs, NJ: Prentice-Hall, 1994.
Tosi, Pier Francesco. *Observations of the Florid Song*. London: J. Wilcox, 1743.
Titze, Ingo R. *Principles of Voice Production*. Englewood Cliffs, NJ: Prentice Hall, 1994.
Trusler, Ivan, and Walter Ehret. *Functional Lessons in Singing*. Englewood Cliffs, NJ: Prentice-Hall, 1972.
Vennard, William. *Singing: The Mechanism and the Technique*. New York: Carl Fischer, 1967.

Voice Therapy
Baken, R. J. *Clinical Measurement of Speech and Voice*. Boston: College Hill Press, 1987.
Boone, D. R. *The Voice and Voice Therapy*. Englewood Cliffs, NJ: Prentice-Hall, 1977.
Boone, D. R. *Is Your Voice Telling on You?* San Diego, CA: Singular Publishing Group, 1991.
Cooper, Morton. *Modern Techniques of Vocal Rehabilitation*. Springfield, IL: Charles C. Thomas, 1974.

Researchers
Because my list of periodicals is long, I have shortened it to include only those presented in the References. However, to begin your research I will list the names of the basic researchers in voice along with periodicals that contain their work. It is a simple matter to look up the articles in the bound volumes of these periodicals in the library.

List of Journals
  Folia Phoniatrica (FP)
  Journal of Applied Physiology (JAP)
  Journal of Acoustical Society of America (JASA)
  Journal of Speech and Hearing Disorders (JSHD)
  Journal of Speech and Hearing Research (JSHR)
  Journal of Research in Singing (JRS)
  Journal of the Nat.l Association of Teachers of Singing (JNATS)
  Symposium: Care of the Professional Voice (SCPV)

Voice (VO)

List of Researchers
Agostoni, Emilio. JAP
Boone, Daniel. JRS
Brodnitz, Friedrich S. JSHD; JNATS
Brown, Oren. JNATS
Cleveland, Thomas. JASA; JNATS
Coffin, Berton. JNATS
Colton, Ray H., and Jo Estill. SCPV
Cooper, Morton. JNATS
Delattre, Pierre. JNATS
Fant, Gunnar. JASA
Fields, Victor A. JNATS
Froeschels, Emil. FP
Gould, Wilbur J. JRS
Hixon, Thomas J. SCPV
Hollien, Harry. JSHR
Karnell, Michael P. FP
Kuhn, G. JASA
Large, John. JNATS; JRS
Lawrence, Van. JNATS
McGlone, R. E. FP
Miller, Richard. JNATS; FP
Petersen, Gordon E. JSHR
Rothenberg, Martin. JSHD; JSHR
Sataloff, R.T. VO
Schlawson, W. JASA
Shipp, Thomas. SCPV
Sundberg, Johan. JRS; JASA; JNATS; JSHD
Titze, Ingo. JNATS
Van den Berg, Janwillem. FP; JASA; JNATS; JSHR
Vennard, William. JNATS

Glossary

A cappella. Without instrumental accompaniment.
Accelerez. Accelerando. Accel. Gradually getting faster.
Adagio. Slow, sustained tempo.
Aggiustamento. Vowel modification. Formant tracking.
Agité. Agitated.
Allargando, allarg. Slowing and broadening.
Allegretto. Between allegro and andante.
Allegro. Lively, rapid.
Allophone. A predictable phonetic variant of a phoneme.
Alto. Also called contralto. Lowest female voice. Rare.
Andante. Moderate walking speed.
Andantino molto cantabile. Rather slow and very songlike.
Animato. Animé. Animated.
Appoggio. Dynamic balance between the inspiratory, phonatory, and
   resonatory systems.
Aria. An elaborate composition for solo voice with instrumental ac-
   companiment, usually from an opera, cantata, or oratorio.
Arioso. Recitative of a lyrical and expressive quality.
A tempo. Return to the first (tempo primo) or previous tempo.
Basso. Lowest male voice. Sometimes with modifiers cantate, profun-
   do, lyrico, Schwarz, Stroh, etc.
Bewegt. Animated.

Cantabile. Singing style.

Cantata. Multimovement sacred or secular composition for voices and
   instruments. Alternates solos, duets, trios, etc. with chorus.

Coda. Literally tail. A concluding, sometimes flashy, passage.

Colla voce. Follow the voice.

Con tenerezza. With tenderness.

Crescendo. Gradually increase volume.{< }

Da Capo (D.C.) Lit. to head. Repeat from the beginning.

Dal Segno al Fine (D.S.-D.S. al Fine) Return to the sign {%} and sing
   to the end (Fine).

Decrescendo. Diminuendo. Decrease volume. { > }

Dolce. Doux. Sweet.

Dynamics. Generic term refers to all intensity directives.

Espressivo. Expressif. Expressively.

Fach. German system defines operatic literature appropriate for specific
   voice types. (for example Kavalier Bariton)

Fermata. Pause. {⌒}

Fliessend. Flowing.

Formant. Area of energy in the vocal spectrum.

Forte. Loud. *Fortissimo.* Very loud. {*f* }{*ff* }

Forza. Force.

Imposto. Placement of the voice.

Interlude. Accompaniment between sung sections of a song.

Langsam. Lent. Larghetto. Lento. Slow.

Langsamer. Plus Lent. Largo. Very slow.

Lebhaft. Lively.

Legato. Tied together. Connect pitches without an interruption.

Leicht. Lightly. *Leicht fliessend.* Lightly flowing.

Lied. Art song in German.

Lungo. Lunga. Long. Long.

Maestoso. Majestically.

Melisma. Vocal passage sung to one syllable.

Melodie. Art song in French.

Meno mosso. Less motion.

Messa di voce. Crescendo and decrescendo on a single note.

Mezza voce. Half voice.

Mezzo forte. Medium loud. {mf} *Mezzo piano.* Medium soft. {mp}

Mezzo soprano. With modifiers lyrico, coloratura, spinto, etc. Medium range of female voice.

Moderé. Moderato. Moderately.

Molto legato. With no interruption between the notes.Very smooth.

Morendo. Dying away.

Opera. Musical theatre work sung throughout.

Operetta. Musical theatre work in which dialogue is spoken.

Phoneme. The smallest unit of speech that serves to distinguish one utterance form another in a language. It may be represented by many different symbols in modern languages, but is represented by just one symbol in the IPA.

Phrase. Musical equivalent of spoken phrase—sentence.

Piano. Softly, quietly {p}. *Pianissimo.* Very Softly {pp}.

Plus. Piu. More.

Poco. Less.

Portato. Phrase articulation between legato and staccato.{⌢}

Presto. Vite. Very, very fast.

Rasch. Quickly.

Recitative. Musical recitation. Declamatory style of singing that precedes an aria.

Refrain. A repeated section of music. Alternates with verse.

Register. A series of notes produced by same mechanism with the same timbre.

Rinforzando. Sforzando. Sudden accent.

Ritard. Retenu. Rit. Ralentir. Hold back. Slowing tempo by increments.

Ritenuto. Immediate reduction of speed.

Rubato. Lit. robbed. To steal time value from one note and add it back to another. Sometimes called *tempo flessibile.*

Ruhig. Serenely. Restfully. Usually quietly.

Schnell. Fast.

Sehr. Tres. Very.

Semplice. Simple.

Spectrogram. Graphic representation of amplitude and frequency of partials in complex sound wave.

Staccato. Articulation using short notes alternating with silence. { ···· }

Straight tone. No vibrato. Tone used in some Renaissance music.

Subito. Suddenly.

Tempo. The speed of a musical composition.

Tenor. Highest of male voices. With modifiers lyrico, robusto,helden, dramatico, comico, Mozart, etc.

Tessitura. The part of the vocal range that is most often used. An aria
  can have high, low, or medium tessitura.
Timbre. Tone color. Formed by varying strength of partials in sound
  spectrum.
Tremolo. Vibrato that is too fast and too narrow.
Vibrato. A vocal ornament which results in an oscillation of pitch 1/4
  step above and below the basic pitch 5 to 7 times per second. It is
  a natural result of the dynamic balancing of airflow and vocal fold
  approximation.
Voce. Voice. With modifiers aperta (open), chiara (clear), chiusa (well
  balanced resonance), coperta (covered), finta (feigned), mista
  (mixed), di petto (chest), piena (full), testa (head).
Wobble. Undesirable oscillation of the singing voice.

Index

About the Author

Richard Davis, baritone, has combined a career as both singer and teacher. After a successful season at Wolf Trap he acquired management in New York City and sang roles in regional opera houses for three years. He sang in a production of *Il Signor Bruschino* in Florence, Italy, in 1989 and has sung five roles with the New Orleans Opera since 1995. As a teacher he has served on the faculties of Columbus College (Georgia), Eastman School of Music (Community Education Division), Nazareth College (Rochester, NY), Oberlin Conservatory, Penn State University, and the University of Southwestern Louisiana. He has published articles in the *American Music Teacher, Journal of Singing,* and the *Choral Journal.* Richard Davis holds the Doctor of Music in Performance degree from Indiana University, and teaches voice and directs opera workshop at Pittsburg State University.